MW01277329

# TOTAL SUBMISSION

—

## TRAINING WARRIORS FOR CHRIST

# TOTAL SUBMISSION

—

## TRAINING WARRIORS FOR CHRIST

MICHAEL PIPER AND PAULA MANGA

DALLAS, TEXAS

Copyright © 2020 by Michael Piper and Paula Manga
www.totalsubmissionministries.com

All rights reserved. No part or any portion of this book may be
reproduced in any form, mechanical or digital, or transmitted without
the prior written permission of the publisher, except for the use of
brief quotations in a book review. Neither the authors nor publisher
furnish any medical advice or prescribe any treatments. It is the
intent of the authors to provide general knowledge to readers to assist
them in their quest for greater understanding and utilization of the
principles presented herein.

Book Cover/Interior/eBook Design by The Book Cover Whisperer:
ProfessionalBookCoverDesign.com

978-1-7353174-0-3 Paperback
978-1-7353174-1-0 eBook


Bible Verses: King James Bible (KJV)


Printed in the U.S.A.

FIRST EDITION

# DEDICATION

We want to dedicate our very first book to the person of the Holy Spirit. He is the One that put Michael and I together in the first place. He is also the person who gave us utterance for this book. So, it is not only dedicated to Him, but it is also His project. We want to thank You Holy Spirit for being so generous and gracious to use us as vessels for these written words. We love You, depend on You, and worship You. We pray that if we can touch one life with the words contained in this book, that the Holy Spirit will give that person revelation and understanding to continue expanding the kingdom of God.

# CONTENTS

# ACKNOWLEDGMENTS

**FROM US:**

We want to thank Betty and Dallas Piper (Paula's mom and dad in love). They have been so essential in the birthing of this book. They have given us encouragement and helped us refine our message. Without their input, we would not have finished this little project of ours. We love you both.

**FROM PAULA:**

I would also like to honor my mother, Inalda Carvalho. Her prayers before she went to heaven, are the reason that I became the woman of God that I am today. Mom, I love you. I miss you and I can't wait for the day that I will see you again. Your loving daughter, Paula Carvalho Manga.

**Ephesians 1:17-23**

"That the God of our Lord Jesus Christ, the Father of glory, may give unto you the spirit of wisdom and revelation in the knowledge of him: The eyes of your understanding being enlightened; that ye may know what is the hope of his calling, and what the riches of the glory of his inheritance in the saints, And what is the exceeding greatness of his power to us-ward who believe, according to the working of his mighty power, Which he wrought in Christ, when he raised him from the dead, and set him at his own right hand in the heavenly places, Far above all principality, and power, and might, and dominion, and every name that is named, not only in this world, but also in that which is to come: And hath put all things under his feet, and gave him to be the head over all things to the church, Which is his body, the fullness of him that filleth all in all."

# INTRODUCTION

## "MY FORMER SELF"

---

### MICHAEL PIPER

**M**y name is Michael Dallas Piper and I wrote this book with my amazing, beautiful, talented and God-seeking wife, Paula "Carvalho" Manga. I want to share with you what Jesus Christ has done in my life. I want to share the transformative power of Jesus Christ and help my brothers and sisters in Christ "walk in victory." **This book is primarily written for someone who is already a believer in Jesus Christ but has not totally submitted (surrendered) their entire life to Him. This is a discipleship book for the person who wants to become a "Warrior for Jesus Christ." This is for the Christian who is no longer happy with "lukewarm Christianity." The Lord said, "So then because thou art lukewarm,**

**and neither cold nor hot, I will spue thee out of my
mouth" (Revelation 3:16).**

If you are not yet a Christian, this book will bring
you to a better understanding of what following Jesus
Christ looks like and what He wants for your life.
Hopefully, it will inspire you to receive Jesus Christ
as your Lord and Savior.

For years, I refused to "submit" my life to Christ.
I lived in "open rebellion" to the word of God. At a
young age, my parents exposed me to Jesus Christ
through Sunday School at the local Lutheran Church.
I could recite the Lord's Prayer at the age of 5 years
old. I went to Sunday School until the 12th grade and
I was "Confirmed" in the Lutheran faith. However,
my bible knowledge/study had very little effect on my
daily life. I would attend church on Sundays and live
just like non-Christians Monday through Saturday.
Although I attended church, there was no change in
my sinful attitude or behavior.

Unfortunately, I was exposed to Playboy Magazine
around the age of 10 and through the next 8 years I
slowly developed an addiction to pornography.

When I entered college, I started drinking and
engaging in premarital sex. I turned away from all
that I had learned at the Lutheran Church. I still
believed in Jesus Christ and I still wanted His provision of eternal life. However, I did not see the need
to change my lifestyle. I felt Salvation was a "free
gift" from God. I assumed that if I believed in Jesus

Christ, I was guaranteed a spot in heaven. There was no real need to change my behavior. I reasoned that God understood that I was just a lowly sinner and I could not really be expected to follow His ways and the "10 Commandments." This seemed an impossible/unattainable request, so I blocked it out of my mind and lived as I pleased.

In addition to drinking and sex, I began to develop a full-blown porn addiction. With the massive amounts of alcohol I ingested, I also started to develop a rage problem. I would let my anger bubble over and literally get out of control. I would start cursing and screaming when I became agitated or someone confronted me. Physical altercations were always a possibility when I was drinking. I would threaten physical violence and berate others. I felt powerful and invincible when I let my anger go overboard. My alcohol-fueled rage had now become my new baseline. I raged with or without alcohol.

It was at this time I began struggling with depression. I was constantly depressed over school, work, relationships and life in general. The more pressure that came into my life, the more depressed I became. The more I drank, the more depressed I would become. I guess this should have made sense since alcohol is a depressant!

Ok, let's recap: on the one hand I was a so-called, "self-professed" Christian and lover of Jesus Christ. On the other hand, I was a raging alcoholic, fornicator, porn addict, depressant with a major anger problem.

I did not respect (and resented) those in authority. I hated the police and the government. I wanted no one to be in-charge of me and I wanted to do whatever I wanted, whenever I wanted. I was a total Hedonist (if it feels good, do it). I was an absolute narcissist. In addition, to all these amazing qualities I was a male chauvinist and a racist. I know you are thinking, "Wow, what a guy"! **I am not glorifying one aspect of my former self. However, I want you to know who I was before Jesus Christ changed me.**

I graduated from college and took all this baggage into the real world and into my 1st of 3 marriages. I married a woman that was not a believer. She accepted Jesus Christ early in our marriage and we did attend church sporadically. However, church was for Sundays and it really did not permeate my life. I was still a heavy drinker with a porn and rage addiction. I cursed constantly and I was extremely depressed.

I would have seasons that I would repent. I might quit drinking and cursing for 6 months. I would reduce the internet porn time temporarily. However, my "clean living" was always short lived. My first wife discovered my porn addiction and I know it was devastating to her and our marriage.

After we divorced, I immediately started another relationship with a woman that was also a non-believer. We were married shortly after my divorce was finalized.

She accepted Jesus Christ and was baptized. I started drinking even more heavily and began getting tattoos. I verbally abused my 2nd wife on numerous occasions and my rage, porn, depression grew to even greater heights. During these years, I built a multi-million dollar retail chain. I had 4 retail stores and over 30 employees. Unfortunately, due to my various issues, I stopped going to work and decided I would rather drink and feel sorry for myself. I lost everything and I eventually declared bankruptcy.

Finally, after splitting with my 2nd wife, I moved from Seattle, WA to Dallas, Texas. I transferred to Dallas with my sales rep job and I knew no one in Texas. I had never been as alone as I was at that time. After two divorces, I was financially devastated. Everything I owned fit easily into a 2- bedroom apartment. My depression, loneliness, anger and porn all came crashing in on me. I had come to the "end of myself." I was done. I was not yet suicidal, but suicide was the next stop. I did not want to kill myself, but I did not know what else to do. I looked up to heaven and said, "Fine, I give up! Lord, do you want my life? You can have my life because I don't want it anymore. Show me what I need to do and I will do it. I just can't live like this one more day!! I SUBMIT"!! At that point, I think I imagined God saying, "Finally! After 50 years of rebellion! Now I can go to work"!!

⸺

WHEN I FINALLY SUBMITTED my life to Christ, I knew

I had to make changes. For starters, I had to stop drinking. I had been drinking hard for 32 years (since I was 18-now being 50). God delivered me almost immediately from this addiction. I was in so much pain that I really could not stand the thought of drinking anymore. It had ruined two marriages and a successful business. Alcohol was the root of all my issues and I knew it. I knew that the only way I could leave my current situation was by abstaining from drinking.

I started going to a nearby church in Grapevine, TX. This biblically-sound church was very friendly and had a great system of getting their members "plugged-in" to serving. I joined their security team and their prison ministry. I began to meet people in the church that really loved Jesus Christ. They loved the church, their pastor and each other. They served and met in fellowship groups and bible studies. These brothers and sisters showed me love and acceptance. They prayed for me and witnessed to me about the love of God. I began to see what a real Christian church looked like. I found the more I got involved and served in the church, the more my walk with Christ caught fire.

I had never participated in prison ministry, but I thought it would be interesting. I always considered myself somewhat gritty/rough and I thought I would be well-suited for this type of ministry. As it turns out, I was well-suited for prison ministry and it has been a major blessing in my life. The more I submitted to the things of God, the more sins and addictions He delivered me from. During the next two years, God totally redirected my path and broke down all the strongholds in my life. During that time, I met a beautiful actress/director/singer from Brazil named Paula Manga. We were married on June 1, 2019. My wife is on fire for Jesus Christ and is a true blessing from God. We are chasing God with all our heart, soul and mind.

My two step-daughters have noticed the radical change in their "Mikey." In fact, my oldest daughter wrote a paper on me for school. When she told me about this paper, I asked her why I had never seen it. She said, "Because it was not a flattering paper as it described, in depth, who you were before you submitted to Jesus." Her explanation quickly ended the discussion with a long awkward pause. However, she added that the reason she started seeking Jesus Christ was the change in me. She said that if it worked for me, maybe it could work for her. Although I was ashamed about the paper she wrote, I was overjoyed by her decision to seek Jesus Christ. My youngest daughter also made the decision to receive Jesus Christ as her Lord and Saviour and both girls have been baptized.

As I mentioned, this book is a discipleship book that is designed to serve as a "roadmap" in breaking down strongholds and walking in victory with Jesus Christ. It is designed to help you stop living in mediocrity and start living for Jesus. To start living the life that Christ has for you and to become who Christ has called you to be. God wants you to be free of sin and addiction.

He came to give you life and life more abundantly. **Jesus did not just come to give you eternal life. He came to transform you and give you an amazing life that will "satisfy" and give you a reason to live. To live for Jesus Christ is the only way to truly live free and have real joy/peace. Money does not satisfy. Relationships and family will not satisfy. Fame and power will not satisfy. Jesus Christ is the only thing that satisfies completely. Everything else is like chasing the wind. This book will show you how to have victory and joy in this life through the power of the Holy Spirit and your personal Walk with Jesus Christ.**

# INTRODUCTION

## "MY JOURNEY TO CHRIST"

—

### PAULA MANGA

I was born in Brazil, in the city of Rio de Janeiro. My beloved mom was the greatest mother one could ever ask for. She was also my role model. She was my example of compassion and selfless love.

In 2007, I came back to Rio after living in America for seven years (Los Angeles). One day my mother came to me and said, "Honey, we are now Christians"! I almost fainted! I said, "Do you mean like that bumper sticker I see that says, "Only Jesus saves?" She said, "Yes darling." WOW!!!! I thought for sure my mom had lost her mind. I had seen my mom's journey in her relentless search for God in various religions and philosophies. From Asian religions to New Age. I always "kind of" followed these religions as well, because as I said, "She was my role model." However, I never really took any of those paths as my own truth. It was my mom's truth. I imitated her out of love. I would do the same with this "crazy Christianity." She invited me (more like persuaded me) to attend church. During the service I would become sleepy and fatigued. I had always worked out at the gym but keeping my arms up in praise (during worship) was way too much exercise for me.

Well, the Word was going inside of me. Over the next six months, strange things started to happen. I would wake up in the morning and it was like scales were coming off my mind (and they were indeed)! I would say to myself, "Of course I came from Adam! Why did I ever think I came from monkeys or from a single-cell amoeba millions of years ago. I was definitely not reincarnated from someone else's life." It sounds funny, but Jesus has a tremendous sense of humor.

Needless to say, it is a personal choice to follow Jesus Christ. I made this choice out of my own "freewill." Jesus was no longer just my mother's truth. He was now my truth as well. **Out of all the paths my mother had walked on (and dragged me with her), we now had the true path. The one and only path of Jesus Christ.** I was baptized in six months. I was in a serious relationship and my boyfriend was also baptized. We decided to dedicate ourselves to Jesus and keep our relationship "holy" until we got married. In 1999, I met this amazing pastor and during our conversation, he explained to me that I needed deliverance. He indicated that I had evil spirits living inside me. I agreed with the pastor, but I did not want those spirits to leave me. Through these spirits, I had used the powers of seduction to my advantage. I did not want to lose this power. I thank Jesus for this pastor's compassion and patience. He waited for the exact right moment to confront these issues. Because he was an M.D. and very cultural, we talked about many things. At some point, he asked me again if I was willing to have these entities cast out of me. For some reason I said yes. Oh boy! The second he said, "By the power of Jesus' name I cast…" I could see myself fading away like I was about to pass out. I did pass out. A few minutes later I woke up not knowing what had just happened to me. He explained that I had been delivered. I left that meeting and for three whole days I could not move at my normal speed. It felt like I was on the moon and I could only move the way astronauts move (very slowly). I studied the Bible and realized I had to be filled now with The Holy Spirit.

⌐

AROUND 2002, MY MOM was diagnosed with cancer of the esophagus and went to heaven in 2004. During this time, my relationship with my boyfriend had ended. I had relocated to another town (Sao Paulo, Brazil) to work with my brother in his TV commercial production company. I then decided that I no longer needed to "go to church" (not because my mom had left me, but because I didn't find a church that I liked). Big mistake!

I was making decent money and things seem to be going fine. However, without a church and without a congregation, I went back to the world. Full force!

Around 2007, two of my dear friends told me that I had become a "very strange drunk." I asked them to elaborate. They said that up until the time I had converted to Christianity (and stopped drinking), I was a "fun drunk." They said that in those days, they would tell me to stop drinking and I would obey. Now something had happened and every time I became inebriated I was, "scary." I had known these friends for 20 years and I was sure they loved me. I knew that they were being truthful in their description of me. I brushed it off and blamed it on my lower resistance to alcohol (I was out of practice). However, their description of my behavior never left my mind. I did admit to myself that at least one thing had changed. I now had "black outs" (where I did not remember a block of time because of my level of intoxication). In the past, before I was saved, I never experienced "black outs." In fact, I was usually the one that was the "designated driver."

It took me another year to understand what had happened. I found this amazing church called, "Snowball" in Sao Paulo (today there is one in LA/Orlando and numerous locations all over the world). One day I came across a certain passage in the Bible that says in Luke 11:24-26: "When the unclean spirit is gone out of a man, he walketh through dry places, seeking rest; and finding none, he saith, I will return unto my house whence I came out. And when he cometh, he findeth it swept and garnished. Then goeth he, and taketh to him seven other spirits more wicked than himself; and they enter in, and dwell there: **and the last state of that man is worse than the first."**

It was as if lighting had hit me. I was that person!!! I had become worse (more worldly) than I was before I was saved!! It's amazing how Jesus in his compassion for us, will use people (that don't even know Him) to impact our lives for Him. My beloved friends had no idea that they were mightily used by the Lord in my life.

At this time, I was delivered again and this time I did not faint during the deliverance. God had mercy on me again! However, it wasn't until 2009 that I went back to Jesus 100%. **This time I was full on for Jesus. Never going back!!**

There is nothing the Lord won't forgive and help us with. What an amazing Savior!!

In 2019, I was married to the most amazing American man. We now serve the Lord together (thus this book). There is so much the Lord has done in my life! I have had so many supernatural experiences and so many blessings that it would take several pages to describe them all. I was a million- dollar sinner. I don't have enough words to express my gratitude for God's immense mercy on my life.

Thank You Lord for everything! I love You beyond words!

# TOTAL SUBMISSION

—

## TRAINING WARRIORS FOR CHRIST

# CHAPTER 1

## WHAT IS TOTAL SUBMISSION TO CHRIST?

—

MICHAEL PIPER

"**Submit yourselves therefore to God. Resist the devil, and he will flee from you**" (James 4:7)

To submit is to come under the authority of something. It could be coming under the authority of a person, entity, organization or government. You are submitting some aspect of your life to this authority. This authority now controls (in some part) either the way you act, think, speak or live. We submit to the traffic laws of our state and to their officials who enforce these laws (police officers). When we say, "Total Submission" we mean "absolute, complete submission or surrender."

**Total submission to Christ is turning your entire**

**life over to Christ and permitting the Holy Spirit to guide your every thought, word and action.** We now surrender our will and we allow God to guide our life. He is now in charge and we are now moving from **"self-centered living" to "Christ centered living."** **"I am crucified with Christ: nevertheless I live; yet not I, but Christ liveth in me…" (Galatians 2:20).** We are now submitting to God's will and His plan for our life.

Total submission is surrendering your life in its entirety. **Total submission is the total commitment to total obedience.** I once heard a pastor say, "Do you know what it will cost you to follow Jesus? It will cost you **EVERYTHING**"!! I did not believe that statement at the time, but now I am 100% convinced that God wants exactly that! **He wants every aspect of your life!** What you say. What you do. What you think about. Who you date or marry. Who you consider friends. How you raise your kids. Every aspect of your job or education. He wants to be included in **everything**. I know this sounds very, very difficult. I know this sounds like an incredible sacrifice. So why should you totally submit your life to Jesus Christ? Good question. Below is the answer.

Luke 9:23-24 says, "And He said to them all, if any man will come after me, let him deny himself, and take up his cross daily, and follow me. For whosoever will save his life shall lose it: but whosoever will lose his life for my sake, the same shall save it."

God has an amazing plan for your life. Amazing! He wants to bless you in every way possible: health, wealth, relationally, family, friends, long-life and ministry to start. **This is not a prosperity message.** I am not suggesting that God will give you a million dollars if you submit your life to Christ. However, I am saying that if you totally submit your life to Christ, He will bless every aspect of your life and give you life "more abundantly"!! However, He will not impose His will on you. He wants you to submit freely to Him and His will. Then He can work in your life and bless you like He wants to bless you. He will direct you in His ways and put you on His path for your life. Let me tell you a secret. Come close . . . listen. **His plan for your life is way, way, way better than your plan for your life! Way better!!**

I have been heavily involved in prison ministry and this is my main message I have for my brothers that are incarcerated. I tell them, "This was not God's plan for your life." "This was your plan." "You chose this, not God." "God's plan is way better and if you submit your life to Him, He will lead you down His glorious path and plan for your life." I have brothers that are getting out of prison and rebuilding their lives with Jesus Christ as their guiding light for their future.

**So why don't we submit?**
When Adam and Eve sinned (by eating the forbidden fruit of the Garden of Eden) we were cast out of the Garden and satan was given dominion over the world.

Satan is now the god of this world and he is the father of sin, immorality and corruption. We are now born into this fallen nature (sinful nature) and a world that satan controls. **The very nature of this world is fallen and rebellious. We are born with a selfish, self-destructive and rebellious spirit.**

An example of this "self-destructive spirit" is when you tell your son or daughter 10 times not to play with the electrical outlet and then find them sticking their finger or a fork into the outlet. Adolescent boys may be attracted to danger or violence. Adolescent girls may be attracted to "bad boys." We are attracted to things that are self-destructive or bad for us (i.e. alcohol, drugs, sexual promiscuity, violence, etc.). People become addicted to these patterns of behavior and consistently repeat these patterns in their lives.

**In addition to having a self-destructive spirit, we are also born rebellious.** "That this is a rebellious people, lying children, children that will not hear the law of the Lord" (Isaiah 30:9). We don't want God telling us what to do or how to live our lives. We don't want to follow His commandments or obey His laws. We want to live like we want to live and do exactly what we want to do. We don't want to submit to our parents when we are younger. We don't want to submit to teachers, our bosses, police or the government. We rebel against authority and so we rebel against God.

**Many so-called Christians profess to believe in Jesus Christ but never let it permeate their daily life.**

**They insist that they are believers in Jesus Christ but deny him with their daily words, actions and attitudes.** They go to church on Sunday and then as soon as they leave the building, they act just like every other person who does not believe in Jesus. Sometimes, these people act even worse than non-Christians. They go to church on Sunday and worship God. Then they live like hell all week. This causes non-believers to look at people that go to church as hypocrites. Unfortunately, many non-Christians use these "hypocritical or pseudo Christians" as an excuse not to believe in Jesus Christ. These non-believers say, "If that is what a Christian 'looks like,' I want no part of that religion."

**So how do you submit your entire life to Jesus Christ?** You start by confessing your sins and turning away from your sins. You confess your belief in Jesus Christ and you accept Jesus Christ as your Lord and Savior. You acknowledge that Jesus Christ died on the cross for the forgiveness of your sins and you ask the Holy Spirit to come and live and reign in you. You accept that the Holy Spirit is now in charge of your life. You now ask the Holy Spirit to teach you and give you wisdom in becoming the man/woman that Christ wants you to be. "Draw nigh to God; and He will draw nigh to you" (James 4:8). We are no longer "self-centered." We are now "Christ Centered." This is the first step in submitting your life to Jesus Christ. The remainder of this book will show you the rest of the steps to fully and totally submit your life to Jesus Christ. **You now**

follow after the things of God and not the things of this world. We become God chasers, instead of world/pleasure chasers. "Yea doubtless, and I count all things but loss for the excellency of the knowledge of Christ Jesus my Lord..." (Philippians 3:8).

⌒

**Chapter Takeaways:**

1. Total submission to Christ is turning your entire life over to Him.

2. We are born with a rebellious spirit because of our fallen, sinful nature.

3. God has an amazing plan for your life that can only be fully accomplished by your total submission to Him and the power of the Holy Spirit.

4. Your Walk with Christ must permeate every aspect of your life.

5. We must stop being "self-centered" and become "Christ-centered."

# CHAPTER 2

## GUARDING YOUR
## HEART AND MIND

—

### PAULA MANGA

When we think of "guarding" something, all kinds of images and situations come to mind, right? For example, if you want to protect your home, you must have locked doors, alarms, watch dogs, security cameras, and if you can afford it maybe even a security team. When people go outdoors (to a park or event) with their little children, they are always on guard watching over their offspring.

People keep their precious possessions (jewelry, gold, paper stock etc.) in a safe or a very protected place. It is never in the open for all to see. In sports, the defense is just as important as the offense (for the former is the one that guards and protects from the opponent to score).

Do you have a friend who really loves their car? They are always taking care of it (making sure it shines, and it is perfectly cleaned). That is guarding.

The Merriam-Webster dictionary has some cool definitions:

"to watch by way of caution or defense: stand guard"

"to attempt to prevent (an opponent) from playing effectively or scoring"

"to tend to carefully: preserve, protect"

"to protect from danger especially by watchful attention: make sure." You get the picture?

We must understand that the Word of God means what He says. Once we have at least three scriptures that back each other up, we must definitely pay attention. It is serious business.

In Luke 6:45 it says, "A good man out of the good treasure of his heart bringeth forth that which is good; and an evil man out of the evil treasure of his heart bringeth forth that which is evil: for of the **_abundance_** of the heart his mouth speaketh."

In Proverbs 4:23 it says, "Keep thy heart with **all** diligence; for out of it are the issues of life." Some other translations say, "above all else keep your heart." Philippians 4:7 speaks about how the peace of the Lord shall guard our hearts and minds.

**Protecting our hearts is a big deal to the Lord.** I believe it's because our hearts harbor our true emotions, our true nature and our true colors. The heart is the organ that pumps all the blood we need to be alive. A person is only considered dead when there is no more heartbeat. It is interesting that God talks about guarding our hearts so much. A person can only speak based on what is in their hearts, even when they don't know it. **I guess it is simple to assume that whatever we let into our hearts will eventually come back out.**

Going back to Philippians 4:7, it says that His peace will guard our hearts. How can we have that peace Philippians is talking about? Only if we know and keep the Word in our hearts, in our minds, and on our lips. Romans 10:8 says that the Word is near us, in our mouth and in our hearts.

If you want to know what is in someone's heart, let them talk for 10 minutes. It will be easy to understand what's in their heart after a brief conversation.

People talk about what is in their soul and what is on their lips and heart.

**The world today is so lost and confused because people take care of their things, but not of their hearts.**

We need to take this very seriously. It is the health of our walk with Christ that is at stake and the health of our lives. I have always been someone who was hurt very easily by the words of others. The Lord has been talking to me about this for quite a while now. It is not to say that what people say does not matter. However, what the Word of God says is much more important. Besides, we know that the enemy will use anyone available to discourage us, bring us down or devalue us. Thusly, it is paramount to guard our mind, soul and heart. If people say something completely out of alignment with the Word, we shall respectably not receive it.

When we hear something offensive or antagonistic, we must immediately forgive and forget. No wonder Jesus said we are to forgive 7x70 (490), in Matthew 18:22. Interestingly, the Hebrew people were put into captivity for 70 years for going against God's command to give the land a rest from its crop on every $7^{th}$ year (7X70).

I imagine Jesus was connecting these numbers to show us that we will be in captivity if we don't forgive. If there is anything you need to let go of, or person you need to forgive, leave it in the past for good. Do it as soon as possible. You are the one who will benefit from this. You will receive peace and rest when you forgive someone. As you forgive, the love of Christ will wash over you. It will help you spiritually, physically, mentally and emotionally. **Unforgiveness, is a poison we take, expecting the other person to die.**

Ok, back to our theme. The world today bombards us with negativity.

The world tells us that we are no good. We are not young enough, rich enough, talented enough, pretty enough etc... This list goes on and on.

When you look around, all you see is billboards,

commercials, movies and news that are magnifying these things. The media never even mentions the heart, ethics, attitude, gratefulness, God, faith, compassion or mercy.

**We live in days that are moving further and further from God and His Word.** It is all about fame, fortune, and power. God sees it very differently. This avalanche in our minds will only make us open to disappointment and heartbreak. That is why the Scriptures keep warning us to guard our hearts. If someone tried to rob you or your house, you would defend it with all you have, right? We must do exactly the same thing with our hearts. It must be a fortress guarded and protected at all times. The enemy will use anything and anybody to pierce through that and hurt us. In Matthew 26:41 it says, "Watch and pray, that ye enter not into temptation: the spirit indeed *is* willing, but the flesh *is* weak." What wonderful advice Jesus gave us. He knows more about us then we know about ourselves. He knew when He said those words that our flesh and our natural minds are easy prey. He said to watch first, then pray. Why? Because we have to be aware and knowledgeable of what is around us or trying to hurt us. Only after we know what the enemy is trying to do can we pray effectively. Prayer is a weapon. However, like any weapon we need to know how to use it accordingly. James 4:2 says, "Ye lust, and have not: ye kill, and desire to have, and cannot obtain: ye fight and war, yet ye have not, because ye ask not."

Wow! What a statement! We must then know how to ask and how to pray.

**Everything changes when you know who you are in Christ and when you have your identity defined in Jesus. It is a game changer.** All that the world tells you starts to diminish and loses its grip on your mind and heart. God does not lie (that is the devil's game).

If the Lord tells us that we need to renew our minds, then that means we are capable of doing it. Through Him. When Jesus answered that a man should be born again (the original Greek would be more like born from above), He was saying that spiritually you are being born from a different kingdom (a different reality). We are no longer in the sphere or realm of the negativity that flows from this world. We flow from the Holy Spirit. As you become this new person in Christ, it will be harder and harder to pay attention and fall for the schemes of the enemy. The enemy becomes something irrelevant and powerless. But again, that is only possible through the renewal of our minds into Christ.

A good exercise is to imagine your heart as the most precious possession you have. Just like a diamond, keep it protected by God's thoughts. Cherish it by God's words, and value it by God's love. He loves you more than words can express. He sent His Son to literally die for you. There is no greater love than dying for someone. If God regards you so highly and puts so much importance on your life, why should you do anything less?

Lastly, the Word assures us that we can, once born again, approach God's throne boldly. **However, if we have condemnation in our hearts, we won't be able to approach His throne with this boldness** (Hebrews 4:15-16). Boldness in the Kingdom of God means a clean heart and a clean conscience. So, get to it! Start working on your sanctification (THINGS YOU RUN AWAY FROM AND RUN TO).

Proverbs 4:23 says, "Keep thy heart with all diligence; for out of it *are* the issues of life." Romans 12:1 says, "I beseech you therefore, brethren, by the mercies of God, that ye present your bodies a living sacrifice, holy, acceptable unto God, *which is* your reasonable service." Romans 12:2 says, "And be not conformed to this world: but be ye transformed by the renewing of your mind..."

**TOTAL SUBMISSION means that you no longer let sin reign in your body. We must discipline our body and capture every thought!** (1 Corinthians 9:27, 2 Corinthians 10:5). This is what it means to Guard Your Heart!

**Chapter Takeaways:**

1. Our hearts are our most precious possessions.

2. We must immediately forgive people when they hurt us and not let the enemy build a root in that rejection.

3. The more we seek the Lord, the more rejec-

tion from the world diminishes and loses its grip on us.

4. We must know how to ask and pray. We must always seek the Holy Spirit because He is the best teacher. We must renew our minds in Him.

5. We must have total dependency on the Holy Spirit, so we will spot it when the enemy is trying to barge into our hearts.

**Pray about it and ask the Holy Ghost to help you!**

*"Holy Spirit, I pray that we get increasingly more understanding of who You are and what You have done for us. We will respect and value who we are in Jesus Christ. We will learn from You how to protect ourselves from the flaming arrows of the evil one, who is using today's society to diminish us. I pray we won't fall into his trap. On the contrary, we will keep our "Shield of Faith" in place and give no room to the enemy's schemes. Help us Holy Ghost walk uprightly with You and become the "more than conquerors" that You died for us to become. Let us see ourselves as You see us. Help us have discernment so we can see when the enemy is coming and we can pray to stop them, in Jesus' name."*

# CHAPTER 3

## DAILY EMPOWERMENT

—

### MICHAEL PIPER

Christians often discuss their "daily devotional." This is a time set aside to study a Christian message and to pray to God. There are numerous daily devotional books that include a short message and a scripture reading. A typical devotional can be completed in 10 minutes or less.

Many Christians have a very difficult time scheduling their daily devotional. They often miss their devotional because of work or family commitments. It is very challenging for these believers to commit 5-20 minutes a day with their Lord.

**The main reason that people have very little victory in their lives in Christ is that they don't spend enough time with their Lord and Creator.** This is why they are constantly full of fear/doubt/anger/sorrow and why their prayers have no power. This is why they are still slaves to sin (steeped in repetitive, rebellious sin). This is why they are still depressed and have no peace. This is why satan still has major strongholds in their lives and why there is no true victory in their lives. These Christians live the same powerless lives that non-Christians live. **I know this sounds harsh, but I am trying to get you to a whole new level with your walk in Christ.** Remember, I said this book was a discipleship book for the Christian that is tired of being "lukewarm." **This book is designed to challenge you and set your walk with Christ ablaze!!** Keep reading and you will understand.

John 14:26 says, "But the Comforter, which is the Holy Ghost, whom the Father will send in my name, he shall teach you all things, and bring all things to your remembrance, whatsoever I have said unto you."

Acts 1:8 says, "But ye shall receive power, after that the Holy Ghost is come upon you: and ye shall be witnesses unto me both in Jerusalem, and in all Judaea, and in Samaria, and unto the uttermost part of the earth."

**I have discovered that to have victory in this life, you must have your "Daily Empowerment." Your "Daily Empowerment" is the power given to you daily from the Holy Spirit.** The Holy Spirit is a living Being that lives in each follower of Jesus Christ. Jesus said that He must leave so He could send the

Comforter(helper) or the Holy Spirit. Your journey in Christ begins with accepting Him as your Savior and Lord. We must accept Jesus as our Saviour from hell and the Lord of our Life. Then we pray and ask the Holy Spirit to come and live and reign in us. We submit our entire lives to the power of the Holy Spirit. Now the Lord has complete control of everything in our life. Our body, mind and soul are now His! We submit every aspect of our life to Him and now through the power of the Holy Spirit, He guides our life. The Holy Spirit will teach us, guide us and give us purpose in our lives. He will help us to understand the bible and give us revelation in our lives. He will help us to understand what God wants in our life and what God's plan is for our life. Each day we must capture every thought, "bringing into captivity every thought to the obedience of Christ" (2 Corinthians 10:5). This can only be done through the power of the Holy Spirit (not by our own self-will).

**Every day we must pray and ask the Holy Spirit for our Daily Empowerment.** Our Daily Empowerment will help us in every aspect of our day. We cannot withstand the attack of satan and his demons without the empowerment of the Holy Spirit. There will be trials and challenges daily. There will be temptations and frustrations. Satan is the god of this world. He uses these trials to get you off your walk. He wants you to be frustrated, depressed and dejected. He wants us to give up and be hopeless.

So how do we get this "Daily Empowerment?" **The only way we can get our Daily Empowerment and fight against the attacks of satan is to "Spend Time with our Lord and Savior."** We need to start every day and begin in worship. Worship ushers in the Holy Spirit, who brings your Daily Empowerment. We need to wake up and get into the Word. We need to listen to our worship music, read our Bible, pray, memorize scripture and let the Holy Spirit fill us up with His anointing, love and power.

As soon as our eyes open in the morning, we need to start praying. Start with just giving Him your love and adoration. Tell Him what an amazing Father and Lord He is. Tell Him how much you love Him and then thank Him. Thank Him for all He has done in your life. Ask our Lord for more of Him and less of you. This is how you should start your day. Then turn on the worship music and PRAISE HIM!! Turn it up to 10 and let the praise music flow! Worship music sets the atmosphere. The tone for the day ahead.

Open up the Word (Bible) and read it aloud. There is power in speaking the Word out loud. Satan and his demons hate the Word and do not want to hear it or be in the presence of someone speaking the Word. Meditate on what it is saying and ask the Holy Spirit to minister the Word to you as you read it. Memorize a verse and meditate on it all day as time permits. This is how you should start your day. **Do not start your day by turning on CNN or Fox News!!! Let**

**me repeat! Do not start your day by turning on CNN or Fox News!!** I believe that news is designed to affect you emotionally with fear, outrage, sadness or lust. If you think about it, that is what every news station/website or paper pushes. "If it bleeds, it leads" (famous expression from a journalist). They want you to keep watching. This is all about "World News." Let me remind you who is the "god of this world"!! Satan my friend!! Our Lord is the God of "Good News"!!

Satan is the "god of this world" (2 Corinthians 4:4) which means he controls this world and the things that influence this world such as news. I highly recommend limiting your exposure to the news by all medias: television, radio, internet, apps and social media. Satan owns all these forms of communication! Satan wants to distract you from God being glorified in your lives. He wants us worried, anxious or caught up in the things of this world and not to be concerned about the things of Jesus Christ. This is why we must guard what comes into our minds and what we focus on. We must guard our eyes and ears.

To get your Daily Empowerment, you need to push into Jesus Christ the first thing in the morning. This sets the tone for your day. Then we must constantly stoke the fire of this empowerment all day long. We must not let satan make us fearful, discouraged or angry during our day. We must stay in the Holy Spirit's anointing presence.

How do we stay in the Holy Spirit's presence? Well,

it's much like what you eat or drink during the day. Let's say you start off your day with a coke and a pop-tart for breakfast. Then a doughnut for a mid-morning snack. For lunch you run down and grab a double burger, fries and a shake. Maybe a candy bar and a mocha in the afternoon. Dinner is pizza and a few beers. Let's say this is how you conduct your food/drink intake 7 days a week/365. What will this do to your body? It's the same thing with your Spirit and Mind. If you fill up your Spirit and Mind with junk (news, social media, gossip and talk shows) you will never build up strength and power spiritually. **If you are feasting on reality tv, romance novels, sports, movies or porn you will never build a strong walk with Jesus Christ.**

I am not saying that you cannot read books or watch movies and sports. I watch movies and I read books. I do not watch movies or read books that focus on things that "rob me" of my Daily Empowerment in Christ. I am sure everyone knows the types of books and movies that I am referring to. In addition, I watch sports (after 27 years in Seattle I still root for the Seahawks). However, if you watch sports 24/7 and never pick up your Bible, it is a problem. Sports has become your religion! Do you scream, clap and raise your hands in the air during a sporting event? Do you do the same during church worship or do you stand with your hands by your side, silently. Hmm. You say you love Jesus? Think about it. Do you really love Jesus?

**A person becomes what he/she meditates and focuses on daily.** Do not believe that you are immune from the attacks of satan in reference to what you watch, read and hear. Satan will use all these medias and all your senses to enslave you. Trust me, no one is immune from his attacks and lies. He is very clever and watches/studies everything you say and do. He knows what tempts you and how to get you off your walk with Jesus Christ. If you focus on the things of Christ, you will become more like Him and less like your fallen, fleshly nature.

As you go through your day, you must "feast Spiritually" on the right things. Listening to hard rock music, rap or country (unless it is Christian) is not going to bring you closer to God. Telling dirty jokes or talking about the bodies of the other sex at the water cooler is not going to "set you on fire" for the things of Jesus Christ.

Everyone has a commute time to work (15 minutes to an hour). This is time for worship music (get a music app), Christian radio station, audio bible or a sermon (from the many church apps available). You can also simply pray. Any of these activities will stoke the fire of your Daily Empowerment. Everyone has a lunch break (another time to be in the Word). Everyone has a commute home. I think you get the idea. The point is that everyone has some time during the day to get with God. There is no excuse for not spending time with God. If you drive for a living, you can spend 3-5 hours a day in the Word. **What would 3-5 hours a day do for your walk with Christ! It would light it on fire!!**

As you do these things, you gently stoke the fire of your Daily Empowerment and you come closer to your Lord. The closer you come to your Lord, the more victory and break through you will have in all areas of your life. The closer you are to God, the less impact and influence satan will have in your life. Satan's power will continue to dissipate day by day as you grow stronger in your relationship and love for God.

The stronger you are in God, the more victory in all areas of your life you will experience. You will struggle less and less with sin in your life. Now you are no longer focused on sin, but you are focused on Him. Your desire for a particular sin will continue to decrease as your desire for Him increases. The more time you spend with Him, the more time you will want to spend with Him. Soon your desire to satisfy your sinful ways starts to diminish. Soon you will find it is considerably better chasing Him then chasing those things you used to chase (the things of this world). **You will find that nothing satisfies like Him.** You will soon be walking less and less in sin and it will be all done through the power of the Holy Spirit (not by your will). It will take less work to resist satan's advances because you will be filled up with Christ. There will be no place for satan and his sinful ways. You will find a peace and contentment that you have never known. As you continue in your walk, you will find true joy that is found in Jesus Christ. **"… for the Joy of the Lord is your Strength!"** (Nehemiah 8:10).

**Chapter Takeaways:**

1.  Each day we must get our "Daily Empowerment" from the Holy Spirit.

2.  Our "Daily Empowerment" from the Holy Spirit is the key to walking in victory in our life with Jesus.

3.  The flame of this "Daily Empowerment" is increased/sustained through activities that focus on Jesus: prayer, worship, bible study.

4.  The more we chase our "Daily Empowerment", the less sin has any place in our life. Satan has no place.

# CHAPTER 4

## DEMOLISHING STRONGHOLDS

—

### MICHAEL PIPER

"**Neither give place to the devil.**" Ephesians 4:27

Give no place to satan! He needs a place to build a stronghold. Only we can give him this place in our lives. Don't do it!

Satan wants to build "strongholds" in your mind to make you a slave to him and stop God from being glorified in your life. Satan wants to paralyze your walk and stop your ministry. **A stronghold is an area of your mind that satan uses to control you.** This stronghold might be an addiction to alcohol, porn or anger. It could also be bitterness, depression, rage, gossip, jealousy, pride or unforgiveness. It might also be an idol: money, sex, job, entertainment, a hobby, a relationship or anything else that someone worships instead of God. Jesus said, "Thou shalt love the Lord thy God with all thy heart, and with all thy soul, and with all thy mind" (Matthew 22:37). You cannot do this if the devil has a stronghold in your life.

You have all heard the scripture Matthew 6:24: "No man can serve two masters: for either he will hate the one and love the other..." This statement is so true! **If there is anything that stands between you and God, it must be removed.** Satan wants to put things in your life that will keep you from seeking God and fulfilling your true potential in Christ. The Lord has a plan for your life and it is amazing! Satan will do anything to distract you from your divine calling. Satan wants to keep you from being truly blessed, as the Lord wants to bless you. The thing that will break down these strongholds is, "total submission" to the Holy Spirit. God does not want you to be a slave to any of satan's strongholds. He wants you to be totally free, so He can work in your life and bless you abundantly in every aspect of your life. These strongholds prevent you from walking into your true destiny in Christ.

"Casting down imaginations, and every high thing that exalteth itself against the knowledge of God and bringing into captivity every thought to the obedience of Christ" (2 Corinthians 10:5).

**Many Christians are not "Spiritually Disciplined." They let sin rule in their lives.** They watch rated R movies with sex scenes and believe it has no effect on their Walk with Jesus. They drink heavily and get drunk. They curse and let foul things come out of their mouths. They do not forgive others and hold grudges. They let anger and bitterness rule their life. They let fear and doubt control them instead of trusting God. They gossip and judge others (pride). They might attend church once or twice a month, (if it is convenient and they have no other plans). They live for pleasure, entertainment, amusement and retirement. They live to accumulate as many material things as possible. They want a big house, beautiful cars, amazing vacations and vacation homes. They search after all this to fill the hole in their heart and the longing in their heart. Their hearts are restless and unfulfilled. They tell themselves just one more promotion and I will be happy. Just a bigger house and I will be happy. Just a better car or boat and I will be happy.

Solomon was the richest king in history. He had many wives, castles, jewels, gold, an army and subjects. He ruled a kingdom. He said, "I have seen all the works that are done under the sun; and, behold, all is vanity and vexation of spirit" (Ecclesiastes 1:14). He tried everything. He said everything is like, "chasing the wind." **We try to fill ourselves up with things of this world. But nothing fills us up except the love of Jesus Christ.** We are hard-wired for heaven. We are in this world, but not of this world. We were meant to be with God. Adam and Eve walked and communed in the Garden with God. That is the way it was originally intended to be. We were not intended to be separated from God. We were designed to live forever with Him. But sin came into the Garden of Eden and we were separated from the presence of God.

When we finally go to heaven, we will be made whole again. Until then, we will always be longing for Heaven. **We have a hole in our heart that can only be filled by Jesus Christ. We can get his kingdom now, but we must seek Him. We must be God Chasers!** We must seek Him daily and chase after Him. Relationship with Jesus must be the most important thing in our lives. Only then can we have peace. Only then will we be content. Only then will we have real joy. Nothing else will satisfy our souls. This is how we must live our lives. Sold out. Totally submitted. Only God.

**One of the biggest weapons that satan uses to bind men and women spiritually is pornography.** Pornography can be a major stronghold in a person's life. Porn is a scourge on our society and our churches. It destroys the porn star actors as well as the people who watch it and the people closest to them. It leads to suicide, failed marriages, depression, anguish, anger, frustration and many other negative emotions. It keeps people in bondage, thusly robbing them of their walk and who they are in Jesus Christ. Satan and his demons are watching our actions and trying to lead us away from Christ. They know they have lost the war, but they want to take as many people to hell with them as they can. Satan does not want God to be glorified in our lives. We must put parameters on our lives. Unfortunately, porn is every bit as addictive as alcohol and drugs. Being a former porn addict, I can speak with authority that I was just as addicted to porn as I was to alcohol. I was addicted physically and mentally. I used porn to "self-medicate" in an attempt to ease my anxieties of the past, present and future. Satan had me trapped in sin. I was his slave and my chains were my addictions (strongholds).

**Alcohol is also a tool of the devil.** Although it is not a sin to drink alcohol, it is a sin to get drunk. My experience has been that even two or three drinks will severely alter one's behavior and drop their inhibitions. Most people will say or do things that they would not do if they were not drinking. My recommendation is to not drink at all. If you must drink, keep it to 1 to 2 drinks maximum. Alcohol will make satan's job much easier. Drinking is another form of self-medication. People use this to manage stress and numb their minds. Pornography and alcohol are both strongholds that satan uses to enslave people.

As I mentioned, porn and alcohol are two major strongholds in peoples' lives. However, these are just two of the numerous types of strongholds. Strongholds come in many forms, such as: anger, depression, drugs, bitterness, pride, regret, sadness, unforgiveness, gossip, jealousy, loneliness and any other condition that enslaves you in the enemy's camp.

Can these strongholds be broken? Can we have

real victory over these strongholds? Take heart my brother and sister in Christ! There is victory available from these strongholds through the power of Jesus Christ! Through the power of the Holy Spirit! There is Victory in the Lord!!

So how can we break these strongholds? Well, the title of this book is, "Total Submission." This is where we start. Start right now. Fall on your knees and pray this prayer:

**"Lord I love you and I confess that I am a sinner and I ask you to forgive me for all my sins. I turn away from these sins and right now I receive you as my Lord and Savior and I receive the power of the Holy Spirit in my life. I confess with my mouth and believe in my heart that you are the Lord. Holy Spirit I ask you to come into my life and take over my life. Take over my thoughts, actions and words. I totally submit my entire life to you. Every aspect of my life I now commit to you. Have your way Holy Spirit. I give you any strongholds and I give you permission to have your way in my life."**

Congratulations! This is the first step in breaking all the strongholds in your life and walking in true and utter Victory in your walk with Jesus Christ.

Now the work can begin. **What you have just declared is that sin and satan no longer have control** or power in your life. You are committed to Jesus Christ and the power of the Holy Spirit.

The key to submitting your life to Christ is this: Your past way of life is no longer acceptable. If you used to get drunk, it is no longer ok. If you used to gossip, it is no longer ok. If you had an unforgiving spirit, it is no longer ok. If you used to curse and rage, it is no longer ok. The old ways have passed. You have made the decision to totally submit every aspect of your life to God and now He can begin the new work in you. He wants to totally transform who you are and renew your mind through the power of Jesus Christ.

Once you have made the decision to submit your life to Christ, you must begin turning over all aspects of your life to Him. **Please understand, I am not suggesting that just by saying this prayer all the work is done. Actually, I am suggesting just the opposite. Saying this prayer is the beginning of the process of submitting your life to Christ.** This is where many ministries miss the mark. They preach that by saying the Sinner's prayer it is finished. Yes, when you say the sinner's prayer you are forgiven from your sins and you are now saved from hell. You will now spend eternity with our Lord and Savior. However, God came to save us from hell and transform (renew our minds) us. We are to walk like Jesus Christ. We are to be imitators of Jesus Christ. This is the beginning of your new life in Jesus Christ.

This process starts by committing yourself to the following:

### Daily time in the Word

Get a Bible and read it. Buy a study guide. Start with the Gospels in the New Testament: Matthew, Mark, Luke and John.

### Worship Music

Listen to worship music (put down the Hard Rock, Metal, Rap and Country Music- unless its Christian). Worship music changes the atmosphere and ushers in the Holy Spirit.

### Join a church

The church you join should be a Spirit-led, bible-based church and you should be able to feel the power of the Holy Spirit during worship and the sermons. Being a part of the church body is a vital component of your Walk with Christ.

### Serve in the church

Get involved in church. Be a greeter/usher. Serve doughnuts. Whatever they need! When you serve you are no longer focused on yourself, but on your brothers and sisters in Christ. Serving in God's church is another form of submission to your Lord. It makes His priorities, your priorities.

### Memorize Scripture

Memorizing Scripture is a powerful tool in breaking down strongholds. Having the Word memorized gives you the ability to bring scripture forward immediately against satan's advances. The word of God is the Sword of the Spirit (your offensive weapon in Spiritual Warfare).

## Join a Bible Study

It is very important to be in a bible study with other brothers and sisters in Christ. **Iron sharpens iron** and we need one another to build each other up in the Spirit. We can help each other learn God's Word and speak into each other's lives. Prayer is a major function within a bible study and there is power when two or more are gathered in His name.

## Tithe

Tithing 10% of our income is biblical (Malachi 3:10) and is not optional. If you have really submitted to our Lord, you will follow this principle. I guarantee God will bless every aspect (including your finances) of your life. Some people say the 10% tithe is only for the Old Testament. If we are submitted to God, we are required to support the church ministry. 2 Corinthians 9:7 says, "Every man according as he purposeth in his heart, so let him give; not grudgingly, or of necessity…" Tithing is another way we show our obedience to God. The level we give is directly proportional to the level of our faith. The apostle Paul encouraged his disciples/churches to give to support the ministry of the Gospel. God loves a cheerful giver!

**Read Christian books**

Reading Christian books is an incredibly helpful way to increase your knowledge of God. This knowledge will bring you into a closer personal relationship with Jesus Christ. There are many excellent Christian authors and you just need to do a Google search to get started.

**Volunteer at a Ministry**

God called us to help the poor, preach to the imprisoned and love one another. Find a ministry that needs help: Union Gospel, Salvation Army, Shelters, Orphanages etc… Wherever there is a need. When you are a blessing to others, you will find that God blesses you even more abundantly. I am not speaking financially, but in that He will bless you with His presence, peace and love. It is really amazing. At Prison Ministry, the guys would always thank me for coming to share the Gospel with them. However, I would always tell them that I am blessed for being allowed to be there with them. Some of my deepest experiences with Christ has been volunteering in Prison. It's amazing when God shows up!

**Bible and Church Apps on Phone**

There are a number of bible apps that you can download to your phone or iPad. **These apps will allow you to read the bible or you can have it read to you with the audio version.** I usually read the bible during my day or listen to it as I drive or eat lunch. Just having the words being read to me ushers in the Holy Spirit.

In addition, many churches also have apps that you can download. **These apps will allow you to listen to sermons and worship music.** There are also devotionals and bible study aids. **I listen to at least one sermon a day.** It will change your entire walk and take you to new levels.

I am constantly filling myself up with the Word of God. Constantly eating/feasting on the Word of God. I fill up daily on Jesus, just like I eat, drink and work out daily.

**This is what turning your life over to Christ looks like. TOTAL SUBMISSION.**

You are now filling yourself up with things of God. Things of the Holy Spirit. Things that edify your soul and bring peace and joy. You are chasing after God and what He wants in your life (instead of what you and your natural mind wants). We must live in the Spirit and not in the Flesh. Faith is a gift freely given by God, but we must exercise our faith every day. DAILY! Not weekly or monthly. Not when you "feel" like it or when it is convenient. This is just like lifting weights or running. The more you lift or run the stronger/faster you get and more stamina that you build.

If you pray or study the Word once a week or once a month you will never build any real faith or true Walk with Christ. It is much like a relationship. If you don't spend any time with the person you want to make a relationship with, you will never create anything meaningful. The same is true with God.

Without seeking Him daily, you will never build a close personal relationship with your Savior and thusly, you will never walk in true freedom from the strongholds in your life.

**We cannot store up today's empowerment for tomorrow or next week.** As the Israelites wandered the desert for 40 years, God provided them with food (manna) on a daily basis. They were instructed to gather just enough food to feed their family for that day. If they tried to save it until the next day, the manna would spoil with worms. The Lord instructed His people to do this for two reasons: first, to make sure they would obey Him and secondly, to show them that He is their daily provider (portion). We must go to God daily to be filled up with His presence and anointing. He wants relationship with us and He wants to commune with us daily. He wants to hear our prayers and worship every day. Then our Lord will be glorified in our life and He will bless all areas of our life.

**Chapter Takeaways:**

1. Strongholds in our life block our relationship with Jesus Christ.

2. The Lord cannot work in our life and be glorified if satan has built up strongholds in our life.

3. To break these strongholds, we must totally submit our lives to Christ and give the Holy Spirit full control in our lives.

4. We must focus our daily activities on things that bring us closer to God: bible study, worship, church, serving, etc.

5. We must run after Jesus daily and make Him the center of our entire life.

# CHAPTER 5

## SPIRITUAL WARFARE

———

MICHAEL PIPER

"**For we wrestle not against flesh and blood, but against principalities, against powers, against the rulers of the darkness of this world, against spiritual wickedness in high places**" (Ephesians 6:12).

Satan is real and he is called the "god of this world." He influences this world through his demons and through people. He uses the internet, social media, hate groups, racism, poverty, tragedies, media, epidemics, money, crime, abuse etc… to turn people away from God. He blinds the eyes and ears of people, so they will not accept Jesus Christ. He blinds people spiritually.

**Make no mistake! We are in a Spiritual War for our souls and the souls of our families and**

**friends.** When Jesus was crucified on the Cross, He broke satan's power over this world. He broke the power of sin and death forever. **"And having spoiled principalities and powers, he made a shew of them openly, triumphing over them in it" (Colossians 2:15).** He broke our chains and set us free. Satan no longer has real power in this world. Satan has read the Bible. Satan knows he has lost and will be eventually cast into the fiery lake forever. He has read Revelations. He knows scripture!! **The only power that satan has in this world is the power that we give him!!** However, he also knows that God made us for Him to be Glorified in our lives. We are to live lives that Glorify our Lord and Savior.

Unfortunately for Christians, satan still has a few goals.

Satan wants to take as many people to hell as he can. He knows he is going, so he wants to take as many souls as possible. If satan can get people to deny Christ and not receive Christ as their personal Savior, they will accompany him to hell.

In addition, satan wants God not to be glorified in our lives. If he can fill us with anger, depression, fear, frustration, sin etc., God is not glorified in our lives. Satan has then won.

As I said, we are in a Spiritual War and I have mentioned some of the tools that satan uses against us. Now let's look at some of the tools we can use against him.

**We have a number of weapons available to us**

that we must use daily to defend ourselves against the attacks from satan.

### Prayer

Prayer is one of the most powerful weapons we have in Spiritual Warfare. We can call on the most powerful being in the universe! Our God and Savior, the Great I Am, the Alpha and Omega, the King of Kings, Lord of Hosts, Yeshua, Elohim, Adonai, Jehovah, Lion of Judah, Abba Father.

We can pray and talk to our Lord! We can give Him all the praise and adoration. There are many ways to pray. One way is to pray the Lord's Prayer and use that as your template:

**Our Father which art in heaven, hallowed be thy name:** Praise Him and give Him your words of love and adoration. Tell Him how glorious and amazing He is and how much you love Him. Thank him for all He has done in your life. Thank Him for every aspect of your life and all His blessings.

**Thy Kingdom Come, Thy Will be done in earth as it is in Heaven:** Pray that His will be done in your life now. Pray to experience His kingdom now and for Him to be Glorified in your Life.

**Give us this day our daily bread:** Thank Him for always supplying what you need and His past blessings and pray for Him to bless you today. Ask Him to bless your family, your business/job and every aspect of your life. Ask Him to work in your life and provide for you what is needed. Make your requests known to Him.

**Forgive us our debts, as we forgive our debtors:** Ask God to forgive you of all your sins (things you have said, thought or in deeds against His commandments). This is also a time where you not only ask for forgiveness, but you repent (turn away) from these sins. God wants you to walk in His ways and obey His commands. If you love our Lord, you will obey His commands. In addition, you need to forgive others that have sinned against you. If we forgive others, God will forgive us. Unforgiveness wrecks people's lives and their walks with Christ. Matthew 6:15 says, "But if ye forgive not men their trespasses, neither will your Father forgive your trespasses."

**Lead us not into temptation, but deliver us from evil:** Ask your Lord to protect you against the schemes, temptations and snares of the enemy. Ask for His provision on keeping you and your family safe from the attacks of satan and his demons.

**For thine is the kingdom and the power and the glory forever:** This is to acknowledge that everything belongs to God and everything is for Him to be glorified. He is to be glorified in this world and in our lives.

**This is one basic outline of how to pray. You can search different prayer styles and guidelines on the internet. The main thing is to pray every day. Start**

**each day in prayer.** Go to a quiet place in your house (many refer to it as a "prayer closet") where you will not be disturbed by anyone or anything. Allow at least 15 minutes to start with. Don't tell me you don't have 15 minutes first thing in the morning. You must make this a priority! Get up early if needed but find the time! This will set the tone for your entire day. Come close to God and He will come close to you. James 4:8 says, "Draw nigh to God, and He will draw nigh to you."

**Start your day in His presence and He will give you all the peace and strength you need to get through your day.** You do not have to overcomplicate these prayers. Just talk to your Father and tell Him what is on your heart and mind. Ask for His provision, peace, strength and presence in your life. Ask Him for protection and covering on your family. Ask Him to bless your job, company or school. Prayer is simply communicating with your Lord and asking for His provision in your life. It's spending time with your ABBA (Daddy) and getting to know Him better. Sharing your deepest thoughts, hopes and dreams with Him. He wants relationship and fellowship with us. Spend this time with Him and you will be filled with His presence. Over time, you will be drawn to spend more and more time with Him.

### Bible Study

We must study and know the Word. Satan and his demons all know the word. They know exactly who

Jesus Christ is. **"And the evil spirit answered and said, Jesus I know, and Paul I know; but who are ye?" (Acts 19:15).** You cannot fight off satan's lies about you unless you know what God says about you. We are heirs, royal priesthood and the same power that raised Jesus from the dead lives in us. We are more than conquerors... "If God be for us, who can be against us?" (Romans 8:31). Satan will lie and accuse. "The thief cometh not, but for to steal, and to kill and to destroy" (John 10:10). You must know the word of God to defend yourself.

You must study every day. It must be like eating or drinking. Would you skip eating for a week or two? When you work out at the gym, you only get stronger if you work out daily. The same goes with bible study. You must feast on the word of God daily. **Jesus said unto them, "I am the bread of life" (John 6:35).** Jesus is the Word and the Bread of Life. You must be in the Word every day and let the Holy Spirit teach you and reveal God's Word. "So then faith cometh by hearing, and hearing by the Word of God" (Romans 10:17). I recommend that you start reading in the New Testament. Start by reading the Gospels: **Matthew, Mark, Luke and John**. The Gospels are all the same story of Jesus Christ told by 4 separate authors. This will give you a basic foundational understanding of the Gospel of Jesus Christ. Keep reading through the entire New Testament and then you can tackle the Old Testament.

In addition, I would get a bible study guide and/ or join a bible study at your church. **I strongly recommend downloading a Bible app on your phone.** Most of these apps will play the bible audibly. You can listen in your car as you drive to work and when you have free time during the day. I have noticed a major anointing in my life just having the bible read over me.

**Our Testimony**
**"And they overcame him by the blood of the Lamb, and by the word of their testimony; and they loved not their lives unto the death" (Revelations 12:11).**

One of the biggest Spiritual Weapons we possess is our personal testimony in Jesus Christ. Every believer has a personal testimony and we are all responsible for sharing our testimony.

As you have read, I have a colorful testimony. I have never glorified my testimony and I am ashamed of who I was before I turned my life to Christ. **However, the first part of our testimony is to convey who we were "before" we submitted our lives to Jesus.** This is not to boast in how bad or good we were. This is to boast of the "Transformative Power and Grace of Jesus Christ."

Here is another secret to our personal testimony: **Genesis 50:20 says, "But as for you, ye thought evil against me; but God meant it unto good..."** Satan desires for us to stay enslaved to sin. God has an entirely different agenda! He takes satan's plan of evil in our lives and uses it for good. He takes our sinful past and makes it a wonderful testimony of His power and love in our lives.

When we share our testimony, we testify to the power of Jesus Christ in our lives. As we tell someone our testimony, they see the Bible in action. We give them a glimpse of what God can do and hopefully they will want to hear more about Jesus Christ. As we tell people about the Good News of Jesus Christ, we must also tell them of what He has done in our lives.

During prison ministry, when the guys and I shared our personal testimonies, something amazing happened. The light of God shined into that place of darkness. Satan's lies and schemes were exposed when we shared our testimonies. We talked about our pasts and how making self-centered decisions (not Christ-centered decisions) took us down the wrong paths. We discussed the schemes and temptations of the enemy. We were led into a deeper understanding of the battle against satan. We witnessed to the power of Jesus Christ and how He broke the power of satan over our lives. Our testimonies also lead us into a more intimate relationship with each other. We learned to trust one another as a brother and fellow Warrior in Christ.

Many Christians are very shy about sharing their personal testimony. They believe that they will be judged or ridiculed. They might feel embarrassed or they may believe these details are too private to share. I absolutely understand and respect this way of thinking. However, we cannot break the power of sin if we don't bring the sin into the light. Satan does his best work in the darkness and in the shadows. When we bring the past sins into the light (with our testimony), the power of these sins are broken.

The second part of our testimony is describing who we are now, in Jesus Christ. We need to speak about how God is transforming us and how He is continuing to change and develop us spiritually. We need to describe how our life has changed now that we have totally submitted our life to Jesus. Tell people of the joy and freedom you now have in your new Walk with Jesus Christ. Tell them what you are now doing for the Kingdom of God. Speak about your new ministry and the victory that you are experiencing in your Walk with Jesus. Again, many times this is an amazing story and will literally shock your audience. They will want to know more of the transformative power of your Saviour.

The third part of our testimony is where God is taking us in our new walk with Him. What does our new future in Him look like? Where is He taking us? What do we feel lead to do in ministry? What is our ultimate goal in our walk with Him?

There is true power in our personal testimony and everyone needs to have their testimony ready to share. Let me address one last thing on personal testimonies. Many people have never lived the life of sin and rebellion that I have lived. I know many Christians that were pastors' kids that grew up in the church and are now leading churches. These people are powerhouses for the kingdom of God. Their testimonies are more powerful because they can testify to what following Christ and totally submitting to Christ will do in your life. These people can testify that if you will submit to the things of God, then God will bless your life and guide you down the right paths. Their testimony is what we should all aspire to be: fully submitted to Jesus Christ from the beginning. Total Submission.

**Worship Music**
**Worship Music is probably the best way to change your atmosphere and usher in the Holy Spirit.** Anointed worship music will open up your heart to the Word of God and help bring you into a real relationship with Jesus Christ. Today's worship music is anointed and filled with adoration/love for our God and Savior! Many of today's most popular music is taken directly from the Bible.

Psalms 84:10: "For a day in thy courts is better than a thousand."

Psalms 96:11: "Let the heavens rejoice, and let the earth be glad…"

Psalms 113:2: "Blessed be the name of the Lord from this time forth and for evermore."

I constantly listen to worship music in my car and at my house. It sets the tone for my day and brings me into the Lord's presence. Worship music keeps my mind and heart focused on the Lord. I suggest you search on the internet for worship music and Christian bands.

This music will absolutely CRUSH you and bring you into the presence of Jesus Christ!

Let the Holy Spirit's presence overtake you. Raise your hands in the air. Close your eyes and listen to the words these bands sing! Look up their songs and print out the lyrics. Find music videos that show the lyrics. Let the words and melodies permeate your mind, spirit and soul. Sing the songs in praise to your Father and worship Him! Fall on your knees and praise Him. Let go! Let the Holy Spirit have His way in you! It's ok to cry and get emotional as the Holy Spirit overwhelms you. It is how the Father shows His love for you. He manifests His presence through the power of the Holy Spirit.

**Memorization of Scripture**
**Having a bible is like having a sword in a scabbard. Memorizing scripture is taking the sword out of the scabbard. Speaking the Memorized Word is using the sword to slay your enemy!** As I mentioned, satan knows scripture. He used it in the Garden of Eden when he questioned Eve about God's command not to eat from the Tree of Knowledge of Good and Evil. He also used it when tempting Christ in the wilderness. How can we fight against satan if he has scripture memorized and we don't? When satan comes up against us, we can quote scripture to defend ourselves and mount a counterattack. For example, if we develop anxiety about a certain situation, we minister to ourselves by quoting scripture. "Be careful (anxious) for nothing;

but in everything by prayer and supplication with thanksgiving let your requests be made known to God" (Philippians 4:6). This immediately comes against the anxiety and replaces it with the powerful word of the Lord. The spirit of anxiety is immediately cast out and replaced with God's command on anxiety. King David constantly quoted scripture and ministered to himself during times of trial. Having scripture at the front of your mind makes satan really weary of starting a fight with you.

Purchase a pack of index cards. On one side of the card write down the entire scripture and on the other side write the book and verse. Try to memorize one or two scriptures a week and keep the cards in a box or container. In 1 year, you will have 50-100 scriptures memorized and it will put you on a whole new level. Just choose a verse from one of your daily bible studies that really speaks to your spirit.

If satan knows you know scripture, then he knows that he cannot distort it with his lies. You are now like a man that not only has a gun to protect himself, but the gun is now loaded and ready to shoot. We are now armed with a Spiritual Weapon to defend ourselves. The Sword of the Spirit is the Word of God.

**Tithing**
There have been many discussions and writings on the issue of tithing. As I mentioned, tithing is a biblical principle. Malachi 3:10 says, "Bring ye all the tithes into the storehouse, that there may be meat in mine

house, and prove me now herewith, saith the Lord of Hosts, if I will not open you the windows of heaven, and pour you out a blessing, that there shall not be room enough to receive it." This is the only time in the Bible where God says, "Test Me on this." He guarantees that He will "open up the windows of heaven and pour out a blessing." Some people say that tithing was only for the Old Testament. However, it is clear in the New Testament that the followers of Christ financially supported the work of the disciples/apostles and the church (2 Corinthians 9:7).

**Giving to the church is a sign of your obedience to God and your love for Him. Remember, we are submitting everything we have to God (including our finances). We can trust Him to bless our life in every aspect (including our finances).**

### Fasting

Fasting is another major tool in Spiritual Warfare.

Acts 13:3 says, "And when they had fasted and prayed, and laid their hands on them, they sent them away."

Acts 14:23 says, "And when they had ordained them elders in every church, and had prayed with fasting, they commended them to the Lord, on whom they believed."

Fasting is designed for us to get our focus off our needs and to focus on the One who provides for all our needs. Fasting helps us refocus on our relationship with Jesus Christ and focus on making Him the center of our life. There are many ways and types of fasting. You can simply fast certain food items or drinks (coffee, soda, sweets etc.). You can fast all food for a time period (24-hour food fast, water only). There are many books on fasting and information on the internet. Be careful not to push your body too hard and talk with your physician if you have medical issues. Again, the internet has a great deal of information on Spiritual Fasting from pastors and rabbis. Fasting is biblical and a powerful tool to get your mind focused on Christ and re-center your walk.

**Speaking in Tongues**

**The Apostle Paul states: "He that speaketh in an unknown tongue edifieth himself…" (1 Corinthians 14:4)**

**Jesus said, "And these signs shall follow them that believe; In my name shall they cast out devils; they shall speak with new tongues" (Mark 16:17)**

**1 Corinthians 14:15 says, "What is it then? I will pray with the spirit, and I will pray with the understanding also…"**

**Speaking in tongues is most definitely a biblical Spiritual Gift.** It is a form of prayer and a form of praise to our Lord. However, many people that have received the power of the Holy Spirit have not necessarily activated this gift. I believe that when you accept Jesus Christ as your Lord and Savior, you then turn your life over to Him. You ask the Holy Spirit to come into your life and you immediately have the power of the Holy Spirit in you. You then have the power of Jesus Christ living inside you. There is nothing more that needs to be done. I don't believe that you need to speak in tongues to have the Holy Spirit move and work in your life.

However, I do believe that there is power in speaking in tongues. As Paul says, it edifies your soul and is your Spirit talking directly to God (1 Corinthians 14:2,4). **Your Spirit is bypassing your mind and speaking directly to God in words that you don't understand.**

In one university study, it was reported that when a person prays in tongues, there was decreased frontal lobe activity to the point of losing self-control. In other words, when you are praying in tongues, you are completely yielding to the Holy Spirit and your natural mind is shut down. In another university study, they found that when you pray in tongues, there was a secretion of chemicals in your brain that were able to boost your immune system 35-40%. The study also observed that there is a part of our brain that is only activated when we are in prayer, praise and worship.

In all my younger years studying the bible, I never received the gifts of tongues. Even after I totally submitted my life to Christ, I did not receive this gift and I was not necessarily focused on this gift.

Two years after submitting my life to Christ, I attended a Christian conference in Fort Worth. I started feeling the desire to pray in tongues. I felt praying in tongues would bring me closer to Christ and I wanted to have this experience. My wife spoke in tongues and several of my best Christian Missionary friends also had this gift. The first night of the conference, the speaker discussed speaking in tongues. I prayed to God for Him to give me this gift and I opened up my heart to receive it. That night nothing happened. I was a little disappointed, but I figured maybe someday God would give it to me.

The next night the speaker had an altar call for anyone with an addiction problem. I was shocked to see between 200-300 men and women go forward. By this point, I had been delivered from my addictions and as we prayed for these men and women I was overcome with emotion. My heart ached for these brothers and sisters that were in bondage to addiction. As we prayed that they would all be delivered from their addiction, I became overwhelmed with love and gratitude to our Lord. I was so grateful that Christ had delivered me from addiction. I was so happy with my newfound life in Christ. I began to weep and I could not stop. I wept through the rest of the service and all the way to the car. My wife asked me what was happening. I tried to explain to her that it was a mixture of intense emotions. I had an overwhelming feeling of love for the brothers and sisters that went forward at the conference. In addition, I felt a wave of gratitude/love to my God for my deliverance and His love for me.

As I started to drive home, I felt the power of the Holy Spirit come upon me. I started to feel a slight twinge or jerk in my neck. Then I started to make really weird, nonsensical noises. It was really bizarre. My wife knew what was happening and she started to video it on her phone (thanks a lot honey!!). This kept up the entire ride home and slowly I was baptized with the gift of tongues. It was an absolutely spiritual experience and I had no control over it.

I believe that the Holy Spirit gave me this gift because I prayed for it and I was purely focused on God and His love for me. I was focused on Him and not the gift. It really is an amazing gift and I pray in tongues daily. Don't get caught up in whether you speak in tongues or not. Let the Holy Spirit guide you in this. Speaking in tongues is an excellent Spiritual Weapon that can be used in your war against the enemy.

**This chapter describes the Spiritual Warfare that we are engaged in daily and the weapons we possess to engage in this war. We are constantly under attack from satan and his demonic forces. We must defend ourselves and wage war against these forces. We must understand this is a spiritual war and we must use the weapons that we have discussed. Prayer, bible study, worship, scripture memorization and fasting are all weapons of Spiritual Warfare. This is how we wage war and this is how we have victory in our Walk with Jesus Christ. This is how we defeat our enemy!**

**Chapter Takeaways:**

1.  We are in a Spiritual War with satan and his demonic forces of evil.

2.  We must use the powerful Spiritual Weapons available to us to fight against satan.

3.  Our Spiritual Weapons include: prayer, bible study, worship music, memorizing scripture, tithing, fasting and speaking in tongues.

# CHAPTER 6

## STEPPING INTO YOUR DESTINY

—

PAULA MANGA

One definition of the word "Destiny" (by Webster's dictionary) says, "That to which any person or thing is destined, predetermined state, condition, foreordained by the Divine."

We see that destiny is something preordained for us, supernaturally by the Lord (Romans 8:29). However, we need to STEP INTO OUR DESTINY. God never intended us to be like spoiled, disobedient children. He wants us to participate in all that He makes available for us. He wants us to be partakers, as the book of Hebrews (2:14, 3:1, 3:14, 12:10, 6:4) tells us. God is so merciful and amazing that He gave us freewill. He gave us the choice to choose Him or not to choose Him. **We must choose to be His. We must choose His**

**route. We must choose to receive His call! We must choose to be chosen!** In Ephesians 1:4,5 God tells us, through the anointed Apostle Paul, that He has "chosen us." **He has called us according to the good pleasure of His will.** However, we still have freewill and we still have to choose His choice.

**Destiny in God has been already designed for us individually.** However, if we don't step into His destiny for us, it will all be in vain. Dr Myles Monroe used to say that the place with the most failed talents was the cemetery. He was right.

Think of it every time you get in your car and go somewhere. You need to know where you are going and the address of that destiny. No one gets into their car and just drives randomly. With the Lord and His plans/destiny for us, it is no different. The Prophet Jeremiah was full of the Spirit when he said, "For I know the thoughts that I think toward you, saith the LORD, thoughts of peace, and not of evil, to give you an expected end." (Jeremiah 29:11) If we don't search and seek God to find that "expected end," we could easily end up in our own "expected end." It is paramount that we seek the face of the Lord. We must cry out for the Holy Spirit to reveal to us our end and our destiny.

In order to step into what God has for us, we must first be filled with the Word of God. The Word of God transforms our minds. If we don't "renew" our minds (Greek word "*metanoiein*" - to change one›s mind or repent), we can't go anywhere with Christ. That is what the Apostle Paul meant when he said, "by the renewing" of your mind in Romans 12:2. He said, "And be not conformed to this world: but be ye transformed by the renewing of your mind…"

**The beginning of stepping into our destiny in Christ, is the renewal of our minds.** He goes on to say that we may prove the good, acceptable, and perfect will of God. This is the will that He has for us. This is that very destiny we have been talking about. You see, God does not move into our realm (He only did that when Jesus became flesh). Now that Jesus conquered all on the cross for us, we must move into His realm. He made it available through the Holy Spirit.

However, we must step into that reality which is unseen. No wonder the Apostle Paul said in Romans 12:2: "And be not conformed to this world." So again, the Bible tells us that there is something other than this worldly realm, this worldly reality we see. However, it is up to us to seek it and find it.

A good friend of mine (a messianic Jewish man) once told me, "God is the God of mysteries who wants to be revealed." How awesome is that!

**God lives and moves in His Word and His Word only. If we want to understand Him, we ought to think like Him. We can only think like Christ, if we know how He acted, moved and thought while here on earth.** The only way of doing that is through His Word. That is why God said in Joshua 1:8 that we should meditate on His Word day and night. Sound too radical? Well than God is too radical… you know why? Because He knew how difficult it would be to change and renew our minds into His.

The mind is one of the most powerful forces in the universe (if not the most). Dr. Caroline Leaf in her book, "Switch on Your Brain" explains that subject amazingly well. It is astonishing to understand the power of our thoughts!

We are so much more powerful than we think. Imagine once we start thinking like God what can happen. I recommend you read her book. It is fantastic to see how science is corroborating with the Bible more and more.

**Stepping into your destiny is going to require faith. Faith is the fuel for a believer. Faith is the driving force to achieve anything with God.** Faith is the material God needs from us in order to move in our lives. In Hebrews 11:6, God tells us that without faith it is impossible to please Him. Think about that statement for a few minutes. God is saying that if we don't have faith, we can't make Him happy or please Him. I don't know about you, but I want to please the Lord with every fiber of my being.

In Hebrews 11:1, the writer opens this chapter with the definition of faith according to God. It says, "Now faith is the substance of things hoped for, the evidence of things not seen." WOW!! Meditate on that thought for a while. God is saying that for us to please Him, we must have a substance of what we want (but do not have it yet) and an evidence of what we don't see. That is powerful and a bit hard to grasp at first. However, when you combine this piece of Scripture with Romans 10:17, "So then faith cometh by hearing and hearing by the Word of God," it starts to make a lot of sense.

**So, if we hear/study/meditate/eat the Word, The Word will begin to change us. We are what we eat. The Word will start to transform us into God's thought process.** We will start to think like He does. Jude 1:20 tells us, "But ye, beloved, building up yourselves on your most holy faith." This is a very clear command. It is in our control to raise up faith in us.

Jesus said in Mark 11:22 that we should have "faith in God" or "the God kind of faith." When God cursed the fig tree, it immediately withered. The disciples were amazed because they did not have the same level of faith that Jesus possessed. Jesus wanted to teach them that they needed this higher level of faith in order to see these amazing results. Once again, we can start tapping into that kind of faith if (and only if) we are Spirit-filled and Word-filled.

One profitable strategy is to memorize Scriptures. However, this is just the first step. We must seek the revelation, the rhema (utterance) of God.

**Once we have a piece of Scripture memorized, we start to seek the Lord on a deeper level for Him to unravel a more profound meaning (revelation) hidden in that passage.** This will take you to a whole different relationship with the Lord, and it will start to peel off layers in your mind. Your mind will start to understand things of God that you never thought of before. One of my favorite scriptures (I have many) is Jeremiah 33:3. This passage says, "Call unto me and I will answer thee, and shew thee great and mighty things, which thou knowest not." He tells us to call out to Him and He will answer. He will tell us great and hidden things of which we are unaware. God does not do anything outside of His Word. **This scripture means that He has hidden secrets in His Word that at first we don't see!**

In 2 Corinthians 3:6, God tells us that the letter kills, but the Spirit gives life. If we only memorize Scripture and not dig deeper, we could fall into that trap. It is the Holy Spirit who brings life and we shall seek Him for those revelations!

### The Corporate Destiny

I call it the "Corporate Destiny" because it is one that every Christian is called to.

Luke 4:18-19 says, "The Spirit of the Lord *is* upon me, because He hath anointed me to preach the gospel to the poor; He hath sent me to heal the brokenhearted, to preach deliverance to the captives, and recovering of sight to the blind, to set at liberty them that are bruised, to preach the acceptable year of the Lord."

We see that this is a calling for everyone. All of us who believe, who are born again, are commissioned to this calling. **We are to preach the Gospel of Jesus**

**Christ to everyone on earth.** Once we are saved, we have been transferred from the kingdom of darkness, to His kingdom of light. We have the Holy Spirit now, on earth. Why? For that reason, to do God's work. This is the great commission. This is the body in action. We are ambassadors of His glory. An ambassador is a legal representative of a particular government. He is authorized to answer for that kingdom. Hallelujah!

Yes, you were uniquely created with a purpose and destiny. There is a unique destiny based on our gifts and grace to fulfill a purpose that only we can. However, there is a destiny that we are all called to fulfill, as a body. Many are called but few are chosen. Why? Because there is an enemy roaming around. Satan heard that you accepted Jesus. He knows that now your destiny is available to you. He wants you to not choose to be chosen. He wants you to stray and he wants to cause confusion. He wants you not to know your identity. **He only worries about you so much because he knows how powerful you are in Christ. He is afraid of your anointing.**

As we just saw in Luke 4, we were all called to those things that Jesus talked about. We are His continuing ministry of healing, deliverance, mercy, prayer and preaching. God will not do this for you. It is up to you to claim that promise and put it into action. This corporate calling does not have to have a platform. You don't have to be famous, have a TV show or be the minister to a small, medium, or large size congregation.

**No, our life is our platform. Our friends, family, or even a complete stranger are the people we are called to do what Luke 4:18 says.**

Remember that in Luke 4:18, Jesus was speaking. However, He also said in John 14:12, "Verily, verily, I say unto you, He that believeth on me, the works that I do shall he do also; and greater *works* than these shall he do; because I go unto my Father."

Notice He never said: "Whoever has a congregation… or… whoever is a minister…or… whoever has a degree in Christian Theology." He said, "whoever believes in Him." Don't misunderstand me. Attending Bible College is great and will help you with your walk in Christ. However, that is not the key. The key is to believe. If you believe in Christ, He expects you to fulfill exactly what He said you could. What I am trying to say is that the homemaker, the lawyer, the teacher, the athlete, the artist, the doctor, the scholar, the student, the retired, whoever you are, can live Luke 4:18. The time for that is now!

Don't waste any more time with things that are only delaying your call. Don't let social media, tv, or anything else rob you of precious time that you could be spending finding your personal destiny and stepping into your corporate one.

Vision is also a very important tool to reach your goal. After all, no one can reach a place where they can't see. The eyes of our inner man (your spirit) has to have a vision of yourself in your destiny. If you don't have a clear vision of your destiny, then start by declaring the Word today. Read the Word, think on it, chew on it and seek His face. You will soon have insight about your destiny.

In Romans 12:3 the amazing Apostle Paul tells us that God gave us a measure of faith. We already have what we need right now. All we need to do is stir up our faith and bring it forth. By faith we believe and we act on it.

**Chapter Takeaways:**

1. We have a specific destiny preordained by God. We must seek Him to find it.

2. We also have a corporate destiny, found in Luke 4:18.

3. Faith is the most important aspect of a believer's life and walk. Without faith, there is no pleasing God, and there is no result or fruit anywhere.

4. Cry out to the Lord with all your might. Seek Him like never before and see what happens.

**Prayer:**

*"Holy Spirit, I pray that You will touch and speak to us, and that we will hear from You and start walking into our destiny. I pray it will be clearer and clearer on what we were put on this earth to do, in Jesus' name."*

# CHAPTER 7

## POWER OF THE TONGUE: LIFE AND DEATH

—

### PAULA MANGA

"The worlds were framed by the Word of God" (Hebrews 11:3).

In Genesis chapter 1, we see the phrase, "And God said" or "And God called" 13 times. This chapter has 31 verses. Almost half of the first chapter we see God "saying" or "calling."

In verse 26, "God said, Let us make man in our image, after our likeness."

God made us in His image and likeness (in Hebrew its "the exact duplication in kind!!). This means that we were made in God's exact "duplication in kind." Since He "made" everything first with His Word (with the declaration that came out of His mouth),

**we can assume that we are supposed to declare and speak what we want to see in our lives!**

During the battle of Jericho, Joshua 1 says that God told Joshua to blow the shofar (Jewish trumpet made of a ram's horn) first and then have the whole army give a loud shout. After the shofar was blown and the soldiers shouted, the walls of Jericho totally collapsed. These great "sounds" (the shofar and shouts from the army) were all that was needed for that particular victory.

I love this Biblical account of Joshua's victory at Jericho. It is so powerful, but we don't usually think of "sounds" making walls collapse.

Joshua was an interesting character. He was a military leader, but also an anointed man of God. He used his military tactics, battlefield strategies and faith. What a combination.

Joshua knew that across the Jordan River was the Promised Land where his ancestor Abraham lived. However, it was occupied by the Canaanites who were larger and stronger then the Israelites. Despite the size and strength of the Canaanites, Joshua had the assuredness that the Promised Land (promised by Yahweh to Abraham) was his inheritance.

The conquering of that land is basically the beginning of Ancient Israel. It gives an idea of how much faith and conviction Joshua had on his rights and destiny. By the prompting of the Lord, Joshua changed his strategy. Instead of regular weaponry, he would use a trumpet. In Joshua 6:20, the Bible tells us that on the seventh day, the walls collapsed. WOW!!! What a moment of trust, faith, obedience and power! I wonder if by the time they were walking around the walls for the second, third, fourth, or even sixth time, they thought how impossible this was. These enormous stone walls collapsed like they had been imploded.

This brings to mind Isaiah 55:8,9 which says, "For my thoughts *are* not your thoughts, neither *are* your ways my ways, saith the LORD. For *as* the heavens are higher than the earth, so are my ways higher than your ways, and my thoughts than your thoughts."

**We must only obey and believe** (no matter how "strange" God's ways might look).

Joshua's story is a marvelous example of releasing the right sound with the right faith. Hebrews 4:2 says, "… but the Word preached did not profit them, not being mixed with faith in them that heard it." This suggests that the Word we hear needs to be mixed with faith.

There is something about the sound that God required of Joshua in order to perform such a miracle. **God will never do anything before we take a "step in faith."** Moses had to be bold and march forward for God to open the Red Sea. Daniel had to be fearless and go into the lion's den. Then God turned the lions into "puppies." Meshach, Shadrach and Abendnego, the three Jewish boys under King Nebuchadnezzer, had to have great faith to step into the fiery furnace. The Lord was there with them and protected them. David had to be strong in his faith to go against Goliath for

God to help him defeat the giant. Esther had to go courageously before the king. The stories go on and on in the Bible.

**What sound does God need you to release today for you to get results in your life? What words should be coming out of your mouth to release God's blessing upon your life?**

I know one thing for sure: it is absolutely related to the Word of God.

It is very clear that God always speaks things before they actually appear. 2 Corinthians 4:18 says, **"While we look not at the things which are seen, but at the things which are not seen."** The latter part of Hebrews 11:3 says, **"so that things which are seen were not made of things which do appear."**

**God CALLED Abram a "Father of many nations."** He was very old and past his natural years of fatherhood, with no children (heirs). How could Abram become the "Father of many Nations" with no heirs? **In addition, God decided to call Abram by a new name.** God changed his name and Sarai's name to Abraham and Sarah. The letter in Hebrew added to his name means "Father" and the letter added to Sarai's name is the letter in Hebrew for "Grace."

I think about how things started to change when everybody around them began to call them by their new names:

Abraham: "Father of many nations"! Sarah: "Grace"!

Romans 4:17 says, "As it is written, I have made thee

a father of many nations, before him whom he believed, even God, who quickeneth the dead, and calleth those things which be not as though they were." **The Lord spoke these things into existence with His words.**

It is amazing how names and words are important to the Lord. Why? Words carry a powerful meaning. Every time the name of Jesus is said, or the Word is proclaimed, the meaning of it is released! Wow!

The Scriptures in Genesis 32:24-26 say that Jacob "wrestled with the angel" and said, "I will not let you go unless you bless me"! We see then that he was not only blessed because he was a fighter (and would not let go until he got his miracles), but also because he DECLARED what he was looking for in God (a blessing).

Jesus made DECLARATIONS over and against the devil in the wilderness (He spoke from the book of Deuteronomy 6:16, Deuteronomy 8:3). His battle was won through His declarations. I truly believe that Jesus could have destroyed the enemy with just a nod of His head or a blink of His eye. But He did not need to do such a thing. Why? Because He was 100% God and 100% man. He wanted to set an example for us. The enemy came to insert words of doubt, unbelief and failure in Jesus' mind. He kept questioning Jesus about what God had said (the exact same strategy he used on Eve).

**Jesus wanted to show us how we win the battles against the enemy. *With words. With words from***

*the Word.* We live in a war of words. Jesus was taken to the desert to be tempted (notice that He only was taken there AFTER He was anointed with the Holy Spirit (Matthew 3:16,17, Matthew 4:1, Luke 4:1). Once you are called by God, the anointing comes through the indwelling of the Holy Ghost. Satan will then come to you and attempt to distort and counterfeit God's Word.

**I'm not saying that to scare you. My goal is to prepare you and train you. An army is only successful when it is able to foresee what the enemy will do. This is how wars are won. Since we know Christ already won this war for us, we just have to be prepared and ready when the devil comes to test us. However, we can be encouraged that satan has no power and he is already a defeated foe.**

When we know our identity in Christ and put our faith into action, everything changes. God tells us to be doers of the Word (James1:22). The Word of God needs a reaction once heard. When you learn something new, have a breakthrough or a revelation, rejoice! Don't take God's things for granted. We serve a marvelous, outrageous, incredible God. React and act accordingly.

**Have you ever wondered why there is a whole chapter in the Bible dedicated to the tongue?** There is no chapter (only verses), dedicated to the heart, liver or lungs(and they are primary organs). God wanted to make sure we understood the importance, the relevance and the power in every word that comes out of our lips.

I am talking about the book of James chapter 3.

In one translation it says that the tongue has dominion and that the tongue is like fire! Wow! Another translation says that the tongue is a world of wickedness!

I love when the Bible uses nature in its amazing analogies. In this particular case, it compares the tongue with a spark that can set a whole forest ablaze! It also says that just as horses need to be tamed, so does the tongue. It goes as far as to compare the tongue to a tiny rudder that controls a huge ship. James 3:9 says that we cannot worship God with our lips and then go and use the same lips to curse somebody. Even though we might "not like" some people, they were still made in the image of God!!!

**What comes out of your mouth is an overflow of what is in your heart. What is your heart full of? Is your heart full of love, purity, goodness and kindness. Is your heart full of hatred, anger, bitterness and lust? Either way, that is what will come out of your mouth (an overflow of your heart). Examine your speech and examine your heart.**

I pray that this is starting to have a great effect on how you use your mouth (just as much as it has been having on me since I began to understand it).

**The power of words+ faith + being in alignment with the Scriptures = miracles and transformation.**

The statement in 1 Peter 2:9 is absolutely amazing and super powerful. It says: **"But ye are a chosen**

generation, a royal priesthood, a holy nation, a pe-
culiar people; that ye should shew forth the praises
of him who hath called you out of darkness into
his marvelous light."

Stop and dwell on that for a minute. **We are "Royalty" and we are a people with complete authority.**
Have you ever seen a king declare something and then
worry if it is going to come to pass? No, he is the king
and he understands his authority. The Bible tells us
that we are, "a royal priesthood", so whatever we say
and declare has to happen. I don't know about you,
but this fills me up with the fear of the Lord when it
comes to the words that I say. **It also prompts me to
speak His Word out loud constantly.**

When I was bitten by the Zica mosquito, the news
and everyone around me said it would be extremely
painful and all my joints would hurt. They said that
I would hurt for at least 6 months and a doctor told
me I would have arthritis. I then decided not to take
any cortisol shots, but I would take BIBLE SHOTS!
I declared the Word all day (Isaiah 53:5). I read the
WORD out loud over and over again. I declared what
the bible says and what the Lord has promised. I was
completely healed in a little over a month! In addition,
I had absolutely no arthritis! No one believed how fast
I recovered. But I knew (and a couple of my personal
intercessors) the reason. My God, my faith and my
declarations of His Word had healed me.

**I believe the Bible is a manual that we should read, learn, and put into practice.**

Have you anything to lose? You have everything to gain! Start right now!

Remember God does not do magic. Sometimes there is a buffering time between the time you declare something and the day that you see it in the natural. Hold on to your faith and to the Word. Declare, declare, declare the Word over you, your loved ones and over any situation.

The year 2020 has been the year of the Coronavirus (COVID-19). This virus has caused an outbreak of respiratory illness and deaths throughout our world. Every country has been affected.

COVID-19 has brought the "spirit of fear" to this world. Every news media and social media is dominated by this subject. So what is coming out of your mouth?

Are you speaking fear: "What if I get the virus and die?" "What if my parents or kids get the virus and die?" "What if millions die?" "What if I lose my job?" "What if all the food runs out?"

Start speaking the following: "I will not get the virus because my Lord will protect me." "No weapon that is formed against thee shall prosper..." (Isaiah 54:17). "Ye are of God, little children, and have overcome them: because greater is he that is in you, than he that is in the world" (1 John 4:4). How about Psalms 91:5,6 which says, "Thou shalt not be afraid for the terror by night, nor for the arrow that flieth by day; nor for the pestilence that walketh in darkness; nor for the destruction that wasteth at noonday."

**We should be speaking the Word and not speaking fear. Quit telling God about the Coronavirus and start telling the virus about your God! My God is mighty! My God is Healer! My God is Awesome, Holy and Worthy of all Praise!**

**Let's examine how you speak to people and what you say.** How do you speak to your husband or wife? Are you edifying your spouse and building them up with your words, or are you breaking them down and crushing their spirit? How are you speaking to your children? Are you calling them smart, beautiful and amazing? Or are you calling them lazy, worthless and stupid? Do you tell your children they are a blessing from God and they will be used mightily for His Kingdom? Speak into your children's lives.

Start training yourself to bless people with your words wherever you go and you shall reap blessings in your own life. How many times do we curse ourselves or somebody else? In traffic? At home? At work? How about when we think we did something wrong? Did you ever call yourself "dumb" or "stupid?" Did you ever call somebody else that? Well, then you are using your lips for cursing yourself or others (cursing words) and that does not glorify God in any way.

I suggest that you write down (at least for the first seven days) all the "cursing words" that come out of your mouth. You will be shocked. This will be difficult but extremely rewarding. Ultimately, you will get to a point that when a "cursing word" comes out of your mouth it will annoy you. That is the sign that the Holy Spirit is nudging you towards the right path. You will begin to exchange these "cursing words" for "words of blessing."

**Chapter Takeaways:**

1. We were made in God's image or exact duplication of His kind. God created all heaven and earth through the words that came out of His mouth. He set this example for us to create our lives in the same fashion (by the words of our mouth).

2. We must learn with Joshua, that there is a specific sound (or words), God is asking of us to release.

3. We are in a war of words. Be very careful what comes out of your mouth.

4. The enemy will try to counterfeit everything God has told us. Be always on guard and vigilant.

5. We are royalty. We should act, think, and speak like it.

**Prayer:**

*"Holy Spirit, we ask You to help us identify and be aware of our words. Give us that nudge every time we say something that saddens You. Give us understanding, knowledge, and discernment to spot the moments when we are about to say something that we will regret. Stop us before we get there and help us see who we are in You. Help us see that we are now the royal priesthood through the blood of Jesus Christ. Amen"*

# CHAPTER 8

## TOTAL SUBMISSION BRINGS TRANSFORMATION, PURITY AND POWER

———

### MICHAEL PIPER

" **A** nd be not conformed to this world: but be ye transformed by the renewing of your mind" (Romans 12: 2).

### TOTAL SUBMISSION Brings TRANSFORMATION

Many pastors and churches are very focused on people receiving Jesus Christ as their Savior and Lord. There are ongoing reports of people making decisions for Jesus Christ. These people are accepting Jesus as their Savior and they are being saved from hell. They are saying the "Sinner's Prayer" and accepting Jesus Christ openly in public. Pastor Billy Graham had millions of people answer altar calls to accept Jesus. Thousands would walk forward at stadium meetings and receive Jesus.

These new Christians are receiving Jesus as their Savior and through their faith in Jesus Christ have eternal life in Heaven. This is exactly what God wants. He wants no one to go to hell and for all His people to go to heaven. That is why Jesus came to the earth. To die on the cross for our sins and for people to believe in Him. "I am the way, the truth, and the life: no man cometh unto the Father, but by me" (John 14:6). People all over the world continue to come to Christ daily and receive Him as their Savior. This is the main goal of the Gospel of Jesus Christ. We are saved through faith in Jesus Christ. Not by works, but by faith in the Son. Ephesians 2:8-9 says, "For by grace are ye saved through faith; and that not of yourselves: it is the gift of God: Not of works, lest any man should boast."

Now I say all this, to say this: **Jesus did not come to us only to die on the cross and save us from hell.** Yes, He died on the cross to give us eternal life for those who believe. However, He also came to break the power of satan and hell. Jesus died on the cross and descended into hell. On the third day He rose again and broke the powers of hell. He made a mockery of hell. He broke the power of death and the power of satan. **"And having spoiled principalities and powers, He made a shew of them openly, triumphing over them in it" (Colossians 2:15).**

**However, Jesus also died for us to be transformed by the renewing of our minds.** He died for us to be changed and for us to imitate the life of Jesus Christ. Now, sin has no place in our lives. If we do not have true change in our lives, we are not stepping into the life that God has planned for us. We must turn our back on sin once and for all. Please don't misunderstand me on this point. **Although we might still go to heaven (if we believe in Jesus, but do not turn from our sins); we are not fulfilling our destiny in Christ. We are not fulfilling God's plan for our life if we are still enslaved to sin. I believe that if we don't turn from our sins(repent), then our Salvation is in jeopardy. Satan wants us to believe that he still has power in our life. He lies, accuses and condemns. He is the great deceiver. However, he has no real power. He only has the power that we give him. Don't give him the power! Trust in your Lord and don't listen to Satan. He is a liar.**

**God wants us to be on fire for Him!**

**"I know thy works, that thou art neither cold nor hot: I would thou wert cold or hot. So then because thou art lukewarm, and neither cold nor hot, I will spue thee out of my mouth" (Revelation 3:15-16).** God wants us to live for Him and for His kingdom. He wants to be Glorified in our lives. He wants us to have power over sin. He wants us to bring others to Christ and He wants us to disciple them in their Walk with Him. **God wants us to turn from**

sin and live a Godly life. **He wants us to walk like Jesus. He wants us to spread the Good News of Jesus Christ.** He wants us to have godly marriages and raise our children in godly homes. God wants His presence to permeate every aspect of our lives. He wants us to love one another like Christ loves us. This means showing God's love through us. We must become vessels for the Holy Spirit to use and to show others God's love. We need to help the weak, sick, imprisoned, impoverished and downtrodden. **Jesus Imitators! Warriors for Christ!**

## TOTAL SUBMISSION Brings PURITY

**When we become obedient to God and His Word, we are submitting to Him. We are submitting to His ways and His path for us.** The more we push into His Word and "Chase Him," the more we develop a thirst and hunger for Him. "As the hart panteth after the water brooks, so panteth my soul after thee, O God" (Psalm 42:1). We begin to develop an appetite for things of God and the things of Heaven. We start to lose our desire for the things of this world. The desires of the flesh and our carnal minds start to disappear. We start to turn away from "things of the flesh" and start seeking "things of the Spirit."

"For Christ is the end of the law for righteousness to everyone that believeth" (Romans 10:4). We are no longer under the covenant of the law. We are under the new covenant of Jesus Christ. We are justified through faith in Jesus Christ. We are made righteous in the eyes of God through our faith in Jesus Christ. We are on our way to heaven. We start to hunger for God and His commands. Before Jesus, we obeyed the law because of the fear of death and the fear of hell. But now we follow the law because we are drawn to the Light of God.

**Before Jesus, we were drawn to the "things of this world." The lust of the eyes, the lust of the flesh and the pride of life. We were drawn to the darkness: sex, alcohol, money, pleasure, greed and power. Now we are drawn to the "things of the Spirit": love, purity, holiness, peace and joy. We are drawn to the things of the Holy Spirit that edify and build up our souls. We are now drawn to the things that build us up spiritually.**

Jesus said, "If ye love me, keep my commandments" (John 14:15). **Now we no longer obey because we are afraid of the law. Now we obey because we love our God and we love His commands. We now want what God wants.** Jesus explained, "My meat is to do the will of Him that sent me, and to finish His work" (John 4:34).

**When we submit to His commands, we discover that His commands are exactly what we need in our lives.**

It is similar to when you tell your child not to cross the street without looking both ways. You are instructing him for his own good (not to exercise your authority over him). You are commanding your child because you love him and you want to protect him from harm. This is exactly how our Lord works. He knows if you follow His commands your life will be better. Your life will be aligned with His will and He can bless your life like He wants to bless you. If you are living a self-centered, sin-filled life, God cannot bless you like He wants to. He is Holy and cannot go against Himself and fully bless you as you live a "sin-filled life." **God needs you to align your life with His will and His commands. Only then can He truly bless you and guide you in His will for your life.**

**TOTAL SUBMISSION Brings POWER**
**When we submit ourselves to Christ, the power of the Holy Spirit reins in our body and mind.** Now we have the power to resist sin. Now we have the power to live a life devoid of fear, anxiety, depression, anger, bitterness, unforgiveness, gossip, sexual immorality, vulgar language, addiction, drunkenness and loneliness. We conquer all these infirmities through the power of the Holy Spirit. Let me be clear here. It is impossible to have true victory over these things through your own strength. Your strength is not enough. But through the power of the Holy Spirit you can have victory over every one of these issues.

**If you let the Holy Spirit control your thoughts, action and words, He will give you the power to be fully delivered from all issues in your life.** The power of the Holy Spirit will give you true victory in all areas of your life. When you align your life with

Jesus Christ, the power of the Holy Spirit will give you Wisdom, Guidance, Strength and Deliverance. This submission also brings power to your prayers. When your life is in alignment with God, He can bless your life the way He wants to bless you. Now you can pray boldly because you know you are walking in the Ways of Christ. When you pray in this power (the power of the Holy Spirit and according to His Will for your life) God is faithful to answer your prayers. "And this is the confidence that we have in Him, that, if we ask any thing according to His will, he heareth us: And if we know that He hear us, whatsoever we ask, we know that we have the petitions that we desired of Him" (1 John 5:14-15). **When you pray in alignment with His Word, He hears your prayer and will answer your prayers. When you pray for strength, health and prosperity He hears you. He will answer. When you pray for healing or wisdom, He will hear you. Now you are praying within His will for your life and with the power of the Holy Spirit.**

**Chapter Takeaways:**

1. Total submission to Christ will allow the Holy Spirit to transform you and set you on fire for Him.

2. Total submission to Christ purifies your heart and fixes your mind on the things of God.

3. Total submission to Christ brings power to your prayers and to your life in Him.

# CHAPTER 9

## THE FIRST WARRIORS

———

PAULA MANGA

**W**arrior -"a person engaged or experienced in warfare, a person engaged in some struggle or conflict" (definition by the Merriam-Webster dictionary).

I researched the subject of Warriors and I found some pretty amazing historical points.

Below are some secular (and not so godly) warriors. However, it shows us how they had certain characteristics similar to our Godly Warriors.

Shivaji Maharaj was an Indian king and warrior that was a master military strategist. He understood the geography of the land and guerrilla tactics. He would raid, ambush and surprise the enemy.

Khutulun was a Mongolian nobel woman, a great warrior, who fought all of her father's battles.

Marco Polo said this about Khutulun: "Her preferred method of combat was to rush into the thick battle, seize upon an enemy horseman, and drag him off to her own people."

Xiahou Dun was a Chinese warrior and legend says that he was hit in the eye by a stray arrow. He took the arrow out, ate his eyeball, and continued to fight (hence his nickname "blind Xiahou, the One-Eyed Warrior").

Genghis Khan was cruel, however, he also unified the tribes in Mongolia. He was responsible for the anti-corruption efforts who sought equal protection under the law of all citizens regardless of status or wealth.

Alexander the Great, during his numerous war campaigns, would educate himself on the territories he would travel. He would study with biologists, zoologists, meteorologists and topologists about a specific area. This knowledge would be invaluable to Alexander when it came time to engage in war to conquer the enemy.

I picked out some words that most of our warriors have in common. They had bailiwick (one's sphere of operations or particular area of interest), determination, faith and discipline. They were all well informed on their enemy. When we look at these warriors, we see a pattern of what a warrior is and how he/she acts. The Bible is full of patterns, templates, and blueprints of how we should behave, if we are in Jesus Christ.

Let's see some of the Biblical warriors.

## OLD TESTAMENT WARRIORS

### SAMSON

The Bible tells us that on many occasions, the Spirit of the Lord came upon Samson and he defeated a lion, multiple enemies and even a thousand men in one of the accounts. He had battle strategies and made his own weapons (Judges 15:4,5). He was a mighty warrior for God because God was upon him. However, Samson did have some issues. Everyone has issues. It shows God's heart and mercy. All the Biblical warriors had problems, but God called them and used them for His Glory! What a God!

### KING DAVID

David was a king. He was a mighty warrior. However, he was not your typical warrior. He didn't look the part. He was small in stature and not very muscular. He was a shepherd. He took care of sheep in the mountains. In 1 Samuel 16, the prophet Samuel came to Jesse's house because God had told him he was to anoint the future king of Israel. However, David's father only brought his tall and well- built sons to the prophet. He did not even think of his son David. The prophet had to ask him if he had other sons. Only then does Jesse call for David. When the prophet saw David, he knew immediately that he was the one that God wanted to rule the holy nation. David was a mighty soldier, a great ruler, and a sensitive poet. No wonder the Bible describes him as, "And when he had removed him, he raised up unto them David to be their king; to whom also he gave testimony, and said, I have found David the son of Jesse, a man after mine own heart, which shall fulfill all my will" (Acts 13:22). David was obedient, like a great warrior should be. In spite of David's shortcomings (and he had quite a few), he was still anointed. This shows us how differently God sees us, compared to how we see ourselves and others.

David killed a lion and a bear in 1 Samuel 17:34-36. God was preparing him to eventually kill the Philistine called Goliath. Against all odds and against the advice from his own family David went after the giant. This giant had been bullying the Hebrew people for forty days (just like Jesus was tempted and bullied for forty days). David charged against Goliath with 5 pebbles. Sounds crazy, right? Not when you are a warrior in God. In God EVERYTHING changes. This includes our weapons and strategies. One thing that speaks volumes to me is what David did BEFORE he ran into Goliath's direction. He first decreed his victory with his WORDS. Why? David understood his enemy and where the battle was about to take place. Just like the secular warriors we have already covered, David knew his enemy. In 1 Samuel 17:1,2 the Scriptures tell us, "Now the Philistines gathered together their armies to battle, and were gathered together at Shochoh, **which belongeth to Judah**, and pitched between Shochoh and Azekah, in Ephes-dammim." This very region, as you just read, BELONGED to Judah. This means that the very territory where the enemy was going to bully the Hebrews, belonged to the Hebrews!! David understood that.

In addition, David NEVER called Goliath by name. He called him "uncircumcised." Circumcision was a ritual that the Hebrew people performed in covenant with the God of Abraham, Jacob and Isaac. He was basically saying that the giant had no covenant with the One true God, therefore, he had no rights to stand on that land. Goliath's defeat was guaranteed. David had absolute certainty that he was going forward in name of the Lord. David knew his victory was assured.

In addition, David had told King Saul the following in 1 Samuel 17:37: "David said moreover, The LORD that delivered me out of the paw of the lion, and out of the paw of the bear, He will deliver me out of the hand of this Philistine. And Saul said unto David, Go, and the LORD be with thee."

David was bringing into his own memory what God had already done for him (we see that in Lamentations 3:21-24).

David understood the God he served and knew his identity in Him. This is a good picture of Christians today. **We must know our territory and our identity. When the enemy comes with his lying words and bullying actions, we charge against him. We declare**

**where we stand, who we are, who we belong to and what God has already done for us.**

**When we speak what God has done in our lives, we work ourselves up in our most holy faith (Jude 1:20). In the Hebrew language, when we give our testimony, we release the same power that was present when that victory took place (it gets loosened again)!**

David went on to become the King of Israel and led the Holy Land into great victories. We can't forget Psalms, the amazing poems/songs he wrote. He understood the power of praise and loving words to the Father. As if that were not enough, he also prophesied through the Holy Spirit (in various Psalms) about Jesus. Read through the Psalms and look for instances that David makes prophetic statements about the coming Messiah. It's fascinating!

## NEHEMIAH

Nehemiah was a slave when God called on him. God commanded him to build the walls around Jerusalem to protect the newly built Temple from enemy attacks. God again chose the most unlikely character for a herculean task.

Nehemiah was determined to build the walls around Jerusalem, despite the great opposition from Sanballat, Tobiah, and Geshem (because they hated the Jews). Nehemiah 2:19,20 says, "But when Sanballat the Horonite, and Tobiah the servant, the Ammonite, and Geshem the Arabian, heard it, they laughed us to scorn, and despised us, and said, What is this thing that ye do? will ye rebel against the king? Then answered them, and said unto them, The God of heaven, he will prosper us; therefore, we his servants will arise and build: but ye have no portion, nor right, nor memorial, in Jerusalem."

Nehemiah understood the unbreakable power of covenant, faith and spoken words. Throughout the first chapter of Nehemiah, we see him fasting and praying. He was a prayer warrior. It makes me think of what Jesus said in Matthew 17:21, "Howbeit this kind goeth not out but by prayer and fasting."

**There are times when we must fast and pray ourselves into our victory. That is why WE ARE WARRIORS. We don't stop. We march forward until we get the victory.**

### ESTHER

Esther was a Hebrew woman, that ends up being chosen by King Ahasuerus (or King Xerxes) to be his queen. Once again, God uses the strangest ways to give His people the victory. The king chose a Hebrew woman without even knowing that he was being used in God's strategies the whole time. Esther becomes a queen and knows she is the one chosen by the Almighty to ask the king to deliver the Hebrew people again (the most persecuted people in the history of mankind). Esther, like Nehemiah and even Jesus, goes into deep fasting and prayer. Then she goes to the king to make her requests for the freedom of her people. Under the strategy of Mordecai, they find favor in God and the king grants Esther's request. Read the whole account of Esther. It is astonishing.

An interesting fact about this book is that it is the only book in the Bible that does not ever mention the name of God. **God wanted us to know that even when it appears that He is not with us, He is. Always. "I will never leave thee, nor forsake thee" (Hebrews 13:5).**

## MOSES

Moses was another unlikely warrior picked by God. It's even a little strange how it all came about.

In Exodus, we learn that Pharaoh (interestingly, we don't have his name) became more and more fearful that the Hebrew people would outnumber the Egyptians. He then ordered the Egyptians' midwives to throw all the newborn baby boys in the Nile river. Moses's mother had a prophetic (but risky) idea. She puts him in a basket and places him in the river close to where Pharaoh's daughter would find him and feel compassion toward him (that is a woman of faith!). Little did she know her son would be the great warrior and deliverer to the Hebrew people. I think about all the ripple effects that occur when we move in faith.

Moses was highly educated in Egypt and grew up with a silver spoon. He had power, privilege and wealth. Still, he never forgot his Hebrew lineage. He never forgot his true identity. For forty years, he was entrenched in the Egyptian culture and lifestyle. Wow, forty years! Think about that. The number 40 is very interesting. Forty years in the desert. Forty days Jesus was in the wilderness. Nothing is a coincidence in the Bible.

Back to Moses.

God was never totally gone from Moses' mind during all that time. The Bible tells us that one day Moses saw a taskmaster beat an old Hebrew man and that did it for him. I imagine that he probably saw that before but for some reason he didn't "see" what was happening until that day. I think God was preparing him for that moment so he would have the revelation of what was going on and act on it. **I wonder how often we "don't see" what God is doing in our lives and think He is not there.**

Moses then kills that Egyptian torturer and buries him in the sand. However, his secret was out very soon. Pharaoh orders him to be killed. He flees to the wilderness. It probably felt like his life was over but it was just the beginning. God has things stored up for us that we can't understand or see (Romans 8:28).

Another forty years would go by before the Lord would redirect Moses' path. I guess God takes His time to fulfill His purpose and to train us to walk in His purpose.

One day Moses sees a burning bush that would not be consumed by the fire (Exodus 3). God calls him and tells him to go deliver his people from slavery. His response was, "What? Me?" Think about this situation.

An 80- year old stutterer/shepherd to go against the most powerful and sadistic man in the known world. He is tasked with telling Pharaoh to set free the very people that are enslaved to do all the manual labor for the kingdom? Well, that is how God works. His ways are higher and His thoughts are higher (Isaiah 55:8,9). Still, think about the faith that Moses had to possess!

I want to lay a foundation to demonstrate how clearly God's ways are different than our ways. So next time you know that God is choosing you, believe it (even if it sounds preposterous). Moses was a major warrior for God and totally submitted to God's purpose for his life. He went on to free the Hebrew people, but it would take another forty years to get them to the Promised Land. He had to deal with the Hebrews' unbelief (Numbers 11:6, Numbers 14:2,3). What a warrior. Against all odds again, God's choice is victorious.

## NEW TESTAMENT WARRIORS

### PETER

Once again, we see God's strange choices. Peter was a Jewish fisherman, whose name was originally Simon. He was not educated or from a royal lineage. He was a simple man. However, Jesus picked him. Peter had issues with his anger. He was hasty but loving and tender. He spoke carelessly quite often (Matthew 16:22, Mark 8:32, Matthew 26:35, John 13:8). He even denied Jesus (Luke 22:54-62, Matthew 26:69-

75). He was the only disciple that walked on water. He was the only disciple whose shadow (although the original translation was more like he was overshadowed by power) healed people. Repeatedly in Scriptures, we see God's mercy on our mistakes, and yet He still uses us mightily. Peter became an enormous Biblical writer, responsible for two letters in the New Testament (1 and 2 Peter). He wrote to the churches in Asia Minor (modern day Turkey). He taught Christians about purity and holiness. He showed them how to rejoice in God amidst persecution. The amount of revelation he received regarding our now Divine nature is incredible. We are now made of incorruptible seed (1 Peter 1:23). He tells us we are now royals, priesthood, and chosen people! (1Peter 2:9). What a great revelation of our new nature.

In the second chapter of 1 Peter, he also talks about complete and total SUBMISSION to God! He says that it is good to suffer for His name and still do good. We have to be totally submitted to live like that. Peter even quotes Isaiah 53 when he says that Jesus took upon Himself our sins, and by His wounds we have been healed.

1 Peter 3:10-17 definitely describes a warrior for Christ. This scripture says, "For he that will love life, and see good days, let him refrain his tongue from evil, and his lips that they speak no guile: Let him eschew evil, and do good; let him seek peace, and ensue it. For the eyes of the Lord *are* over the righteous, and his ears

*are* open unto their prayers: but the face of the Lord is against them that do evil. And who is he that will harm you, if ye be followers of that which is good? But and if ye suffer for righteousness' sake, happy *are ye*: and be not afraid of their terror, neither be troubled; But sanctify the Lord God in your hearts: and be ready always to *give* an answer to every man that asketh you a reason of the hope that is in you with meekness and fear: Having a good conscience; that, whereas they speak evil of you, as of evildoers, they may be ashamed that falsely accuse your good conversation in Christ. For *it is* better, if the will of God be so, that ye suffer for well doing, than for evil doing."

This scripture is incredible. Peter understood how disciplined in the Lord we have to become.

In the final chapter of letter two, he says something that is astonishing: "But, beloved, be not ignorant of this one thing, that one day is with the Lord as a thousand years, and a thousand years as one day." (2 Peter 3:8)

It is easy for us to read that over and over again and not fully appreciate what he is saying. But he got the revelation of Heaven with God being outside of time and he explained it brilliantly.

## THE APOSTLE PAUL

Talking about an unlikely choice. I think Paul is the most unlikely of them all! Think about this for a moment. Paul was a gun for hire, a hit man, a professional murderer of Christians!!! But again, God sees every-thing very differently and in an almost weird way.

In Acts 8, it says that Saul (the Hebrew name and Paul is the Roman name) was destroying churches and approved the killing of Stephen. Stephen was a deacon who did great wonders and miracles (Acts 6:8). Saul was highly educated. He had a Hellenistic education. He spoke not only Hebrew, but also Greek. He was also born with a silver spoon. He was a warrior. He was a Roman citizen. But he was 100% Hebrew and proud of it. This guy was respected, feared, and applauded.

Saul was on his way to a city called Damascus to capture more Christians and bring them to Jerusa-lem as prisoners (many to be executed). But then he had an encounter! It dramatically changed his life forever. In Acts 9, we read about this light and Jesus appearing to him and asking why he was persecuting "Him." Interestingly, Jesus never asked Saul why he was persecuting Christians. He asked Saul why he was persecuting "Him." Paul (formerly Saul) then becomes just as aggressive to save as he was to kill. **It's amazing how the Lord takes the carnal person we were before receiving Him and now uses that person to bring Glory to His name. Like us, Paul was a warrior for darkness and now became a Warrior for Christ.** I think of how people probably doubted and didn't be-lieve in his newfound Christianity. Sound familiar? Did you experience that same attitude from others when you got saved? It comes with the territory. Paul wrote

13 books (or letters) of the New Testament, plus the book of Hebrews (most scholars believe he wrote it). This warrior journeyed throughout all of Asia Minor and Greece. He was relentless and amazing!

In Acts 16, we see Paul and Silas being beaten with rods, flogged, imprisoned and their feet fastened with shackles. In addition, he was imprisoned in Philippi, Jerusalem, Antipatris, Caesarea and on a ship across the Mediterranean (Acts 23, 26).

Paul would go on and write the following letters:

Romans/1 Corinthians/2 Corinthians/ Galatians/ Ephesians/Philippians/Colossians/1 Thessalonians/2 Thessalonians/1 Timothy/ 2 Timothy/Titus/Philemon.

His handkerchiefs also healed (Acts 19:12). Isn't that surreal? He was so full of the Spirit, and dead to himself: "I am crucified with Christ: nevertheless I live; yet not I, but Christ liveth in me…" (Galatians 2:20).

In 2 Timothy 4:2, Paul tells us to be ready to preach the Gospel (in season and out of season). I think of an Olympic athlete who will train whether they want to or not. Their focus never weakens.

Prison could not hold Paul back. He wrote amazing revelations in prison! One of my personal favorites is the letter for the Ephesians.

Ephesus was a city in Asia Minor. Paul is writing to non-Jewish people and telling them they have the same opportunity as the Jews to know Jesus and be saved! This was groundbreaking because most people thought that knowing the Messiah was only for the Jewish people.

One of the many revelations that Paul had in prison was one regarding the armor of God. He noticed the amazing armor that the guards wore. He was given the revelation that we as Christians also have an armor for spiritual warfare that we must put on. In Ephesians 6, he describes this whole armor from head to toe. Only warriors need an armor!

Ephesians 6:10-17:

"Finally, my brethren, be strong in the Lord, and in the power of his might. Put on the whole armour of God, that ye may be able to stand against the wiles of the devil. For we wrestle not against flesh and blood, but against principalities, against powers, against the rulers of the darkness of this world, against spiritual wickedness in high places. Wherefore take unto you the whole armour of God, that ye may be able to withstand in the evil day, and having done all, to stand. Stand therefore, having your loins girt about with truth, and having on the breastplate of righteousness; and your feet shod with the preparation of the gospel of peace; above all, taking the shield of faith, wherewith ye shall be able to quench all the fiery darts of the wicked. And take the helmet of salvation, and the sword of the Spirit, which is the Word of God."

Do you see it? Do you realize that there is an armor

we are supposed to put on everyday? Imagine a soldier, engaged in a war, dressed in civilian clothes. He has no helmet or body armor. He would certainly set himself up for defeat. We are the same in the invisible realm. We are in a war, thus weapons and armor are necessities. God knew this and has provided for us in this area. Christianity is an "offensive lifestyle." We charge against the enemy. We overtake him, subdue him and destroy his presence in our lives. Thank you Lord for equipping us with this armor and weaponry!

Paul had the Roman Military in mind when he wrote this Scripture. They were masters of the sword and spear in combination with the shield. They had the most expensive weaponry and armor on the planet. They were highly disciplined and masters of weaponry. They were fierce, relentless, savage, unyielding and unstoppable. They were loyal to their Emperor. They met their opponents on the battlefield with only one outcome in mind (victory)! They trained for hours, days, months and years. If they did not train hard enough, the price would be their life (as their enemies would overwhelm them).

This is how we must fight spiritually! We must fight with only one outcome in mind! VICTORY!!! We must train, learn and become masters of the Sword of the Spirit (God's Word). We must use our "Shield of Faith" to extinguish the fiery darts of the enemy!! We must protect ourselves from all the attacks of the enemy!!

I suggest reading the book written by Rick Renner

called, "Dressed To Kill." He is a teacher of the Greek language and explains this armor in great detail.

**The biggest warrior of all times: JESUS CHRIST OF NAZARETH**

**Jesus was the biggest warrior on earth. Warrior of God. Warrior of the people. Warrior of salvation. Warrior of life. Warrior of love.** No doubt about that. You may say, "But He was not an odd choice, He is the Son of God." Are you sure he was not an odd choice? Let's take a look.

The people of Israel were waiting for the Messiah. However, they were looking for a Messiah that would go into battle and destroy their enemies. Jesus went against all that they thought "The Savior" was supposed to be and act like.

It shocked the Jewish people when Jesus told them to pray for their enemies and love others because God is love. Then He was also required to die for humanity?? What?? Then He was born in this "pathetic" little town of Bethlehem? (Matthew 2: 5-6)… be pierced for us (Isaiah 53:5)….chastised for us?? Now do you see why Jesus was an unlikely and strange choice for God to use to accomplish His grand plan? He chose Jesus to correct all that happened in the Garden of Eden.

Loving who hates you is such a far-fetched idea to our natural senses. It is almost degrading. However, the King of the universe was all about that kind of love.

**"Christianity is the only story where the hero dies for the villain."** WOW! What a great way to describe Jesus. I don't know who made this quote, but they were right on the money!

This is why Jesus is such a revolutionary figure. Dying for someone else is already almost impossible to think about. Dying for someone that doesn't deserve it or for someone that dislikes you, is way too much to accept. Well that is Jesus. Only someone with amazing strength could turn the other cheek to their enemies (Matthew 5:38-40).

Only in Christianity, is the religion "THE PERSON." Jesus said in John 14:6, "I am the way, the truth, and the life: no man cometh unto the Father, but by me." Isn't that phenomenal? I mean Jesus is saying that He is the religion. He is the doctrine. He is the path. In Mark 10:45 it says, "For even the Son of man came not to be ministered unto, but to minister, and to give his life a ransom for many." What a God we have and serve!

**When we look at Jesus' life, it is so flabbergasting and beyond our imagination, to see a man who was born to die. To die for us. His life is a testament of His total commitment. His absolute discipline. His amazing devotion. His unrelenting obedience. He was beaten, betrayed, whipped, spit on, slapped, pierced, tortured, cursed, disfigured, mocked, humiliated and hung on a tree. Just to name a few things that happened to Him.**

Yet, He was faithful to His calling. He remained true to the reason He came to earth and all out of love for us. His loving compassion to heal and set people free was unending. **However, He said all of the events of His life and death happened because He permitted it.** In John 10:18 Jesus said, "No man taketh it from me, but I lay it down of myself. I have power to lay it down, and I have power to take it again. This commandment have I received of my Father." He obeyed the Father out of His own freewill. **In Matthew 26:53,54 it says, "Thinkest thou that I cannot now pray to my Father, and he shall presently give me more than twelve legions of angels? But how then shall the scriptures be fulfilled, that thus it must be?" The Biggest Warrior!!**

He alone fulfilled prophecy after prophecy about the Messiah in the First Covenant. Here are just a few:

Zechariah 12:10, Isaiah 53:5, Genesis 3:15, Psalms 2:6, Psalms 2:7, Psalms 34:20, Exodus 12:46, Numbers 9:12, Micah 5:2, Malachi 4:2.

In the book of Revelation it says that Jesus will return. The description given by the Apostle and Revelator John is astonishing and magnificent!

In Revelation 19:11-15 he says, "And I saw heaven opened, and behold a white horse; and he that sat upon him was called Faithful and True, and in righteousness he doth judge and make war. His eyes were as a flame of fire, and on his head were many crowns; and he had a name written, that no man knew, but he himself. And he was clothed with a vesture dipped in blood: and his name is called The Word of God. And the armies which were in heaven followed him upon white horses, clothed in fine linen, white and clean. And out of his mouth goeth a sharp sword, that with it he should smite the nations: and he shall rule them with a rod of iron: and he treadeth the winepress of the fierceness and wrath of Almighty God."

**If that is not a picture of the greatest warrior, I don't know what is.** When Jesus was hanging on the cross he said, *"It is finished,"* and he bowed his head and gave up the ghost" (John 19:30). **The most amazing warrior won the battle for us! It has been won! Do you understand that? As warriors for Christ, we just have to ENFORCE that victory on earth. Preach the Gospel, telling people the Good News!** However, only a fighter has what it takes to carry out this mission of Jesus Christ. The enemy knows when someone does not understand how this battle works. In Acts 19:15 it says, "And the evil spirit answered and said, Jesus I know, and Paul I know; but who are ye?" That is amazing! The enemy can tell when the person does not know who they are in Christ! We have to work at entering this new identity of a warrior who has already won, but still has yet to enforce the victory!! If you understand this concept, it will transform your life. That is why Jesus came to earth as a man. He saved us and made us a whole "new species" of people. We were made for His "good pleasure" and for Him to be Glorified in our lives.

I could continue on with many more Biblical giant

warriors such as: Abraham, Joseph, Rahab, Samuel, Jeremiah, Isaac, Gideon, Enoch, Phoebe ( we would not have the letter to the Romans if it wasn't for her), John, Peter, Priscila and Aquila, Junia, Timothy, Stephen, Mary and Joseph. All these warriors were afraid, doubtful of their abilities and incredulous when God picked them. The same with you my beloved reader.

**In the Hebrew language there is no word for coincidence. You are reading this book for a specific reason. God is calling you. If all these men and women answered the call, then so can you. As long as you understand that all this can be accomplished through God and the power of the Holy Spirit (not in your strength, but His).**

Once again, I need to make something very clear. There is one huge difference between the secular warriors that I pointed out in the beginning of this chapter and the Biblical ones. Secular warriors served themselves and Biblical warriors served God's purpose. The secular warriors functioned in ego and the Biblical ones in faith. The secular warriors moved people through fear and the Biblical warriors moved people in hope. The secular ones fought with ambition and the Biblical ones in calling. Self-serving purposes motivated these secular warriors, but for us Biblical warriors, "Kingdom Business" is our fuel.

I just wanted to show that there is a protocol, template and pattern amongst all these warriors. They had the drive, determination, discipline and courage despite their fear.

We are entitled with the privilege to be God's warriors. However, our fight is His and our battle is not against people, but against the spirit realm and the forces of evil.

The first disciples faced great difficulty because of the large number of "gods" around the world at that time. The Galatians, Romans, Greeks, Ephesians, Corinthians and Phoenicians all faced completely different looking gods. They were all the same deity, but with various shapes and names! These "gods" were everywhere. The Romans had naked gods, the Phoenicians had gods that looked like they came from a horror movie, and the Greeks had pretty looking gods/goddesses, to name a few. All these entities were in charge of that world at that time. For more information on these "gods" I suggest reading, "Battles of The Elohim" by Apostle Dr. Christian Harfouche.

The same authority that the first church walked in, we walk in. The book of Acts does not have an amen at the end. Why? Because it is still happening today, through us. The same power Jesus bestowed upon them, was bestowed upon us. The great commission is still the same. The same enemy that was against them, is against us today. Although fallen, demons are still angels. This means they don't multiply or die. They don't get tired and they never stop pursuing/attacking us. I don't want to scare you, but since you are reading this book, I assume you are a warrior. At least you have something inside of you that tells you so. Like the warriors we have studied here, you must know and understand your enemy. More importantly, you must know and understand your position in Christ.

**Chapter Takeaways:**

1.  We are in a spiritual war, whether you like it or not.

2.  We are warriors in Christ and for Christ. He already won the war, but we are still His enforcers.

3.  We have to be in the Word and seek His face so we can be transformed into His image.

4.  We must Pray, meditate on the Word and fast.

5.  Think about your new nature and dwell upon what the Word says you are now.

6.  We become what we behold. The more we behold Christ, the more we become what He says we are.

**Prayer:**

*"Our Father, help us through the agent of the Holy Spirit, understand our position and understand all that was accomplished through the work of the Cross. Expand our minds to really understand the mind of Christ. Help us die to ourselves, our agenda and our own desires. Let us be in alignment with your plans*

*for us. Gives us the strength and determination to fulfill our warriors' calling. Gives us discernment to see when we are not drenched in your Word enough in order to be transformed. Help us to be hungry and in desperate need of Your Word. In Jesus' name, Amen."*

# CHAPTER 10

## THEY WILL KNOW WE ARE
## CHRISTIANS BY OUR LOVE

———

### MICHAEL PIPER

"A new commandment I give unto you, That ye love one another; as I have loved you, that ye also love one another. By this shall all men know that ye are my disciples, if ye have love one to another" (John 13:34-35).

"Master, which is the great commandment in the law"? Jesus said unto him, "Thou shalt love the Lord thy God with all thy heart, and with all thy soul, and with all thy mind. This is the first and great commandment. And the second is like unto it, Thou shalt love thy neighbour as thyself. On these two commandments hang all the law and the prophets" (Matthew 22:36-40).

**Loving your neighbor edifies your soul**
In April of 2017, I attended a Christian Conference

that taught about the love of Jesus Christ. Here is what I personally took away from this conference: **"Everyday, show Christ's love to other people." We must be a vessel for Christ to show His love to others through the power of the Holy Spirit. This conference changed my life.**

I learned that we must show Christ's love to others daily. We need to pray for people and speak into their lives. Each day we should minister and prophesy to our brothers and sisters in Christ. We should do this wherever we go. Look for an opportunity to bless or encourage others. Show others that you love and care for them. Buy someone's coffee and just tell them you want to bless their life. Look for a chance to show God's love. As you shop for dinner at your local grocery store, look for people to bless. Buy their groceries or pray for them. When you bless people in this way, it floods them with the love of Jesus. Trust me, this is a rush! You will also be extremely blessed by this experience. People will be shocked at your behavior because most people don't do these things. **In today's society, people are too caught up with their own lives. They are too busy to worry about showing God's love to others. Even people that are highly religious and knowledgeable about Jesus Christ, show no love toward people they see or meet in public.**

**Christ wants us to love one another like He loves us.** He first loved us while we were still sinners (before we accepted Him as our Lord and Saviour). We obey this "love commandment" because He has instructed us to do so. However, when I started doing this on a regular basis, I discovered something amazing! With each conversation I started, or coffee I purchased, I was overwhelmed with love from the Holy Spirit. After each interaction, the Holy Spirit blessed me immediately with His love, presence and embrace. It is an amazing and powerful way to live.

In addition, **showing Christ's love to other people is addictive! The more you do it, the more you want to do it.** I love showing Christ's love to others. Plus, it's really easy! I have no agenda on each interaction. The Holy Spirit does all the work. All I have to do is be present and be faithful to reach out. I just have to be willing to follow the prompting of the Holy Spirit. I simply say, "Hi, how are you today?" "Are you having a good week?" I will ask them if they have a prayer need. I might say, "Hey, do you know about Jesus Christ?" "Do you go to church?" It really does not matter how you start the conversation and everyone is different. It's all about showing Christ's love to others. If this is your only thought, it frees you up to just relax and concentrate on the person. Let the Holy Spirit do His work!

**Remember the Great Commission: "Go ye therefore, and teach all nations, baptizing them in the name of the Father, and of the Son, and of the Holy Ghost" (Matthew 28:19).** Sharing the Gospel of Christ and His love is very simple. When you are open to showing Christ's love to someone (in a way previously discussed) they will be curious. They will say, "Hey, there is something about you. What is it?" Then you say just one word: "Jesus." Immediately, you now have a captive audience. Someone who is asking you about Jesus and His love. It's that easy. This is not a complicated formula. Show Christ's love and let the Holy Spirit do what He does. Honestly, you and I cannot bring people to Christ. Only the Holy Spirit can bring people to Christ. It's the Holy Spirit's job to convict and bring people to Christ. It's our job to love and follow the prompting of the Spirit. It's our job to share the Good News of Jesus Christ! I have heard people say to me, "I can see Jesus in you." Trust me, I know it's not me they see, but the Holy Spirit within me. However, it is still pretty cool to hear people say that they see Jesus in me. Conversely, with my former self, I have heard people say, "I see evil in you." I prefer the former statement!

**Giving to the poor shows Love**

Homelessness is an epidemic. Before I totally submitted my life to Christ, I was afraid of the homeless guys with the cardboard sign. I wanted nothing to do with them. They sickened me and scared me. I never looked at them or gave them a dime. That has now all changed for me. When I walk or drive by people holding cardboard signs, I stop and ask them their name. I tell them that I love them and that more importantly, Jesus Christ loves them. I give them my personal testimony and I pray over them. Then I give them a small tract (booklet) of the book of John with a $5, $10 or $20 bill slid inside one of the pages. These people are usually shocked and overwhelmed. They don't expect that kind of love from a stranger. People that are homeless don't expect someone to ask them their name and tell them they are loved. They certainly don't expect someone to pray for them.

In most cases, when I start praying for homeless brothers and sisters, they start crying. When I am finished, they are grateful and their faces have changed to joy and peace. It is really an amazing experience. I know many people will say, "What if they use the money for alcohol or drugs?" My answer is: "I don't care"! It is not my job to judge what they do with the money I give them. It is my job to love on them and show mercy. "He that oppresseth the poor reproacheth His Maker: but he that honoureth Him hath mercy on the poor" (Proverbs 14:31). "He that giveth unto the poor shall not lack: but he that hideth his eyes shall have many a curse" (Proverbs 28:27). I know many of you may not have homeless in your neighborhood or where you work. However, you can volunteer at the Union Gospel or the Salvation Army. Trust me, there are plenty of people in need. Again, this is an amazing ministry and you will be blessed beyond measure.

**Prison Ministry shows Love**
**"Naked, and ye clothed me: I was sick, and ye visited me: I was in prison, and ye came unto me" (Matthew 25:36).**

I started prison ministry in April of 2017 through my local church. I had never done any kind of real ministry. However, I always thought Prison Ministry sounded very interesting. Considering my former life was all about being tough and mean, I thought prison ministry might fit me. When I started to go into the prison I was scared. It was intimidating. However, the more I worked with the guys and showed Christ's love, the more I was blessed by this ministry. It was amazing worshipping and praying with these brothers in Christ. In addition, it was not just me preaching and sharing Jesus with them. Many of these brothers knew the Word better than me. Many times, they were praying over me and giving me Words from God. **Iron sharpens iron!** I never had any agenda when I went into the prison. I just wanted to show God's love to my fellow Christian brothers. Every time I did prison ministry, I was blessed and walked away amazed at our Lord's love for us and His provision.

**God has commanded us to love each other. He wants us to show others His love through the power of the Holy Spirit. If we truly love God, we will show our love to Him by obeying His commandments. If we truly love God, we will love our brothers and sisters and share the Gospel of Jesus Christ.**

**Chapter Takeaways:**

1.  God has commanded us to love each other.

2.  Showing love to each other edifies our soul and showers us with His love and presence.

3.  We are to show God's love to each other daily.

4.  We need to show love to the poor and imprisoned.

# CHAPTER 11

## BROTHERS IN CHRIST/SERVING

———

### MICHAEL PIPER

Before I submitted my life to Christ, I had very few friends. I mainly had drinking buddies (except for one friend that is still like a brother to me today). I did have a couple Christian Missionary friends that I knew in Seattle. I spent very little time with these brothers as I felt ashamed of the sinful life that I was living. These Christian brothers never once condemned me and always prayed for me. However, I couldn't shake the feelings of guilt and shame. I was very isolated, lonely, restless and bored. I would drink to numb these things and self-medicate. Then the drinking would lead to pornography, anger, depression and despair. **Isolation is one of satan's biggest weapons. If satan can isolate you, he can really harass you with his**

**lies and accusations. He can also use the isolation
to tempt you. He can use this isolation to bring
depression, sadness, loneliness, anxiety and despair.**

I never really trusted most people (that was another
reason I had few friends). I felt that friends were not
really a necessary part of life. I had my wife at the time
(now ex-wife), my one friend, my alcohol and my porn.
I watched a lot of television and basically that was my
world. I really did not want anyone else in my life. I
had my mother, father, brother and sister-in-law but
they all lived 2000 miles away. I saw them 3 or 4 times
a year and spoke with them on the phone regularly.

**When I finally came to the "end of myself," I
was divorced and alone in Dallas (where I had re-
cently located from Seattle). I was totally isolated,
miserable and probably pre-suicidal. Something
had to change!**

I started going to a nearby church and signed up to
serve in their security and prison ministry. I met a great
group of guys on the church security team. We trained
together and worked each Sunday to protect our pastor
and our congregation. We trusted and relied on each
other and it was amazing getting to know these men
of God. As I mentioned, I joined the Prison Ministry
at the church and met another great group of brothers
and sisters who love Jesus. We got to know each other
as a team as we went to the prison to minister together.

I also joined the Men's weekly bible study. I started
meeting the men of the church and I was amazed at

the love and support that I received. I started to spend time with these Christian men and they started ministering and speaking into my life. As I mentioned, I never wanted any friends (especially Christian friends). I thought that the Christian men in churches were boring, judgmental and lame. I discovered that the men in the church were nothing like I had envisioned. Actually, I found out that it was I who was boring, judgmental and lame! I found these Christian men to be very encouraging, understanding and supportive. My new Walk with Christ opened up a whole new world of Christian brothers in Christ.

I started going to church every week and attended other church activities and bible studies. I started going to lunch and dinner with these men of the church and God spoke to me through these men. My feelings of loneliness and despair started to dissipate. My Walk with God started to grow and my understanding of the importance of having brothers in Christ started to become real. We studied the Bible together and prayed over one another. These friendships I started to make were different than my previous friendships. These relationships were more intimate. We could share our deepest thoughts and emotions. We could cry, be vulnerable and say, "I love you." I trust these men and developed strong ties with them.

The difference with these relationships was Jesus Christ. Our friendships were based on Jesus Christ. This was the center of our friendship and brought us almost instantly to a deeper, more intimate brotherhood. It let me know that I was no longer alone and that someone else cared and prayed for me. These brothers changed and enriched my life with their friendship and love. Over the last couple years these friendships have continued to grow. My three closest friends and I meet every week for lunch and fellowship. We talk about our jobs, our wives and kids. We discuss our struggles and triumphs. But most of all we talk about Jesus Christ and what He has done in our lives. This is our common bond and what keeps our group tight and together. We are also accountable to each other and we make sure that we are all on the right track and pushing into our relationship with Christ.

It is important to have brothers that you are accountable to and who can call you out if you are getting "off track" in your Walk with Christ. You need a brother who will pray with you and help redirect your course. We need to be able to submit to one another and let our Christian brothers speak into our lives.

I also have my bi-monthly bible study that has 10-13 guys. We again talk about our lives and families. We pray over one another and we study the Word of God together. It is amazing what the Holy Spirit does at our bible study! **Iron sharpens iron!** We build each other up in the faith. Having brothers in Christ reminds you that you are not alone and that others struggle with the same things that you do. Having one of my brothers pray over me is one of the most powerful weapons I have against satan. We bind the hand of satan together and we release the blessing of Jesus Christ in our lives. There is power in having Christian brothers and this brotherhood is a major weapon in our Spiritual Warfare.

**Mentoring**

It is vitally important to your walk with Christ to have a mentor and to be a mentor.

In the New Testament, the Apostle Paul wrote the books 1 Timothy, 2 Timothy and Titus. Timothy and Titus were both disciples or mentees of Paul. He was their Father in the Spirit.

**Having a mentor gives you someone to assist you in following the correct path for your Christian life. This person will encourage you and guide you in your Walk with Christ.** In addition, this person will keep you accountable and can help to correct you if you start to drift in the wrong direction. Your mentor can also help to direct your study and the direction of your ministry. Just as Christ submitted to the will of His Father, we must submit to God and to each other in Christ. We must be vulnerable to each other and submit to each other in Christ. We need to allow others to speak into our lives and minister to us. There is power in having a mentor and letting this person help guide you on your path in Christ. Of course, it is vitally important to make sure you get a mentor that loves and knows God intimately. Your mentor needs to know the Word of God and live the Word of God.

This is an important decision in your walk as I believe your mentor needs to be Spirit-led and grounded in the Word of God. Mentors are an important aspect of growing in your faith. We should constantly be moving to the next level in our Walk with Christ. If we are not moving forward in our Walk with Christ, we are moving backward. There is no neutral. A good mentor can assure that you are constantly moving to the next level in Christ.

**It is also very important to be a mentor.** This is a big responsibility and not one that should be taken lightly. When you mentor someone, you must be very careful that you are Spirit-led and that you know the Word of God. You cannot advise someone on their walk if you don't know the Word. In addition, you must also be walking as an imitator of Jesus Christ. If you are not walking closely with Christ, it is difficult to advise and guide another believer. In addition, a mentee will be not only listening to what you say, they will be watching how you live. Your actions speak way more than your words. If you are walking in the ways of Jesus Christ, you can fully advise and instruct your mentee through the power of the Holy Spirit. It is a true blessing to become a mentor to a fellow brother in Christ. As you pray and minister to your brother, God blesses you both with His presence and love. I love mentoring brothers in Christ.

### Discipleship
**Luke 6:40 says, "The disciple is not above his**

**master: but every one that is perfect shall be as his master."**

**John 8:31 says, "Then said Jesus to those Jews which believed on him, if ye continue in my word, then are ye my disciples indeed."**

**Discipleship should be a major focus of the church.**

Discipleship in the church is the teaching and study of the Word. It is the practical application of daily following and imitating Jesus Christ. After we receive Jesus as our Lord and Saviour, we must dedicate ourselves to studying and teaching the Word of God. We must learn what the Bible says about us and how we are supposed to live. Then we must teach it to others and help build up the other members in the church. The Bible will give you constant revelation and wisdom. The more you study the Bible, the more the Holy Spirit will talk to you and guide your life. Discipleship is done through learning from each other and studying the Bible. Discipleship in the church is vital in creating a healthy and powerful church. We cannot just go to church on Sunday and expect to learn everything we need to know. We need to be constantly in the Word with other brothers and sisters in Christ. We should have bible studies and discipleship programs for all the men, women and children in the church. Discipleship is how we build up strong believers to push forward the Kingdom of God. To have real revival in the church, we need Discipleship.

**Chapter Takeaways:**

1. We are not meant to be isolated. We need brothers and sisters in Christ in our lives.

2. By serving in the church and attending bible studies, we can build powerful Christian relationships.

3. To take our Christian Walk to new levels, we should have a mentor and ultimately become a mentor.

4. We need discipleship in the church to create a strong and growing body.

# CHAPTER 12

## TOTAL SUBMISSION CONCLUSION

—

### MICHAEL PIPER AND PAULA MANGA

We hope that this book will inspire you to live "on fire" for Jesus Christ. This project came from our hearts. We deeply desire to see the body of Christ set ablaze, doing the same works as the early church. We pray that the words on these pages will leap out and enter your spirit like an atomic bomb.

We want to challenge you to stop being lukewarm in your Walk with Christ. We want all the strongholds in your life to be broken down. We want you to walk in real power and victory. In addition, we wanted to give you a "roadmap" to fully submitting your life to Christ and living the life that God has called you to live. Then we want you to take this same message to your family, friends, neighbors, church, strangers, nation and ultimately the world! This is our desire to see people changed and for this change to spread like a wildfire!

We are privileged and honored that you took the time to read this book.

**Please believe this: everything we told you to do or not to do, we apply in our lives every day.** The Christian Walk is a never ending, amazing journey. We are being transformed. It has been a blessing to have you partake in our experiences and revelations.

May our beautiful Lord Jesus bless you, keep you, and shine His face upon you.

We love you. Very much.

Mike and Paula

# AUTHOR BIOS

Michael Piper and Paula Manga were married on June 1, 2019. Since the day they met they have Chased God together. They live in Dallas, Texas along with their puppy Charlie Chaplin. Their ministry is to help Christians move from being "lukewarm" to fully "ablaze" for Jesus Christ. They have started a Discipleship Ministry that they hope and pray spreads like wildfire. They want you to be blessed by this book and they want you to know that they love you and pray for your life in Jesus Christ.

CPSIA information can be obtained
at www.ICGtesting.com
Printed in the USA
LVHW040819280920
667265LV00004B/273